To Bill He

May this

blessing to you.

*Chuck Wilson*

# THE
# ROAD
# HOME

# THE ROAD HOME

BY
CHUCK WILSON
*and* DEBBIE WILSON

MILL CITY PRESS BOOKS

MCP Books
2301 Lucien Way #415
Maitland, FL 32751
407.339.4217
www.millcitypress.net

Printed in the United States of America

Edited by MCP Books

ISBN-13: 9781545612552

"...and may you live to see your children's children."
Psalm 128:6

To our granddaughters, Addison, Aubrey and Layla

# PREFACE

I love to quilt, so it's only natural that I look at my life from the perspective of a quilter. Beautiful quilt designs are crafted from pieces of different fabrics sewn together. I love to look at the colors, feel the textures, study the patterns, and imagine different hues lovingly pieced together to construct a quilt top. My favorite part, however, is hand stitching the top layer through the middle layer of batting to the underside of the quilt to complete the project. Each quilting stitch reflects determination, and forbearance. For me, it's like leaving a part of my very soul to warm someone—something tangible that will remain intact, and give pleasure to others long after my life on earth has passed. I picture myself continuing to quilt throughout eternity while I consider the generations of descendants who may find comfort as they wrap up in one of my projects.

As I reflect on my life, with its joys, challenges, and struggles, I see my varied personal experiences as pieces of a quilt. The quilting *thread* that holds it all together, and keeps the layers from shifting, is my father in heaven who has showered me with blessings. It's time I share the patchwork of my life with others in the hope they too will find the peace and assurance only God can provide. Hopefully my story, and faith journey, complete with mistakes and imperfections along the way, will bring the reader to the realization there is nothing a God-centered life cannot endure.

Debbie Wilson

# TABLE OF CONTENTS

# CHAPTER 1

# CROSSROADS

### *(Chuck)*

T*hud*. Debbie's knees slam into me—broadside.

"Ouch."

She is naked, and straight-from-the-shower soaking wet.

"Feel...there's a lump! Found it while taking my shower."

"What?"

"It's cancer, I know it is," she almost screams.

Her trembling hands guide mine. There, my fingers distinguish the marble-sized mass within her left breast. Fear tingles from fingertips to brain—displacing exhaustion. Worst-case scenarios wrestle against thoughts of reason.

"It can't be..." I insist.

Thin streams of water flow onto my face, arms, and chest from Debbie's saturated brown hair draping over me. Turning in the current without my glasses, I squint to read 5:12 a.m. on the bedside clock. How long have I slept? I climbed into bed at 2:00 a.m., but couldn't sleep. One hour...maybe. I wish I could reverse time; be waking from a bad dream. Yesterday was the worst day of my life—now this. What the hell am I going to do?

My mind flails for something brave to say, to keep us afloat.

Instead, all I can say is, "It's okay, honey...everything'll be okay."

*(Previous day)*

"Stupid, stupid…why did I ever leave the Navy?" I think and sigh a gravelly sigh aloud while shaking my head like Lurch from the old *Addams Family* TV series.

Pissed off and desperate, I'm enduring a long day of interviews for a job I do not want. It's getting late. I'm killing time alone—seated at a gray steel desk in what will be my office if hired. The cell is windowless. Scenery consists of a mountain range of file cabinets, capped with faint peaks of folded blueprints. The clouds beyond are shelves of white technical manuals for emergency generators, and high-volume air conditioning systems. Unlike the paintings by Bob Ross on his PBS series, there are no happy little trees or a snug cabin nestled in a valley with smoke curling out of the chimney.

My headhunter is scraping the bottom of the ugly-job barrel. He made it clear if I do not give my best performance to land a position as Assistant Director of Facilities at this hospital, he will drop me as a client. The salary, if hired, will be less than half of what I had established as my absolute bottom line.

It's mid-fall, and November's nasty-cold is just one more thing that sucks in my life. My search for a job, which began in early spring—when I still had that new MBA smell—has produced no prize.

Blaming October's infamous stock market crash, known as "Black Monday," for my woes does not hold water. My fellow naval officers, with whom I worked as an Assistant Professor of Naval Science these past two years, sailed smoothly into nice corporate positions with their MBAs. They are on course, rocketing into the future while I have failed to launch. Fact is, I'm not trying hard enough. My heart isn't in it.

Three years ago, my longtime dream to earn a master's degree in writing unraveled like a cheap Tijuana blanket. Turns out, full-time work as a college professor teaching English and writing is a very tough gig to get. Further, even if I were hired by some junior college somewhere, I would not be able to support my family financially in the manner I desire. Salaries commanded by those elusive and coveted positions are paltry. Visions of sporting corduroy jackets with patches on the elbows among my fellow academics evaporated. Prospects of spending summers and holiday breaks writing great American novels slipped below the surface. Getting an MBA was my best path to leaving the Navy, and leaving the Navy was my overriding objective.

Farkle—my nickname in high school—comes to mind. The Farkle Family was a long running skit on the old comedy series, *Laugh In*. This job resembles the career I want as much as the red-haired Farkle children favor their dark-haired parents in appearance. The kids all echo the freckles and bright ginger of the happy neighbor, Ferd Berfle. Was Mr. Farkle oblivious to the obvious or did he choose to ignore the painful truth of his wife's long-term affair with Ferd? Why am I considering the motivations of Frank Farkle? At least my kids resemble me.

This office is below ground level in an area without the manners of false ceilings. Here in the bowels of the building, pumps and motors whirr while back-up systems stand ready. Where are the sweaty, bare-chested men shoveling coal into open flame? They must be taking a break. A network of naked pipes, air ducts, and electric cables crisscross over my head, conduits for the brute forces of power, air, and fluid on their way to places in the building with the bland aesthetic comfort of suspended ceilings.

It's as if I have returned to my stark existence on board a warship. There are two worlds on a ship. Life topside, which includes watching the ship's bow cleave the sea in half, and the ever-widening trailing wake. Considering the pitch and roll of the day's ride against the vast ocean and sky is a wonderful thing, but the reason I am in the running for a job overseeing a hospital's facilities is my extensive experience in the world below deck. Much of my time while on sea duty was spent in that steel-world without windows where activities essential to propulsion and producing every other type of power and service a ship requires take place. As an engineering officer, I was in tune with the alignment of gas-turbine engines, electric generators, motors, pumps, boilers, and evaporators. Changes in sounds and vibrations, conveyed through the metal decks beneath my feet, informed me of everything.

It was out of fear that I became one with the ship. The prospect of the ship going cold and dark at sea haunted me. Being towed back to port destroys a ship's reputation. Such a failure would change my outlook, and lower my opinion of myself. So, out of pride, the loss of a vital tonal from the din of shipboard noises would cause me to jerk awake from dead-sleep. If something was wrong, I felt it in my bones. Solving problems gave me great satisfaction, and I ran to trouble with excitement. The enlisted men held me in high regard. They saw me as part of the solution, not the problem—as was the case with most officers. My issues were with fellow officers, especially those above me in position, which was probably a result of my coming from nothing compared to the more well-to-do backgrounds of most of my peers.

"Respect the position regardless of whether you respect the person," I was advised by friends trying to keep me from self-destructing.

I both loved, and hated my military life. Don't see how I could ever come to love this job as Assistant Director of Facilities, should I be so fortunate as to get hired. Civilian life does not at all resemble my dreams. My stomach churns sour. The vacant nameplate slot on the open office door stands ready to grip my name. The muscles of my jaw and lower back seize.

Today has been a series of meetings with perfectly nice muckety-mucks in the hospital's hierarchy, and walking tours through the labyrinthine innards of massive medical buildings—areas rarely seen by anyone not carrying a toolbox.

It was 2:00 a.m. this morning when my alarm went off to begin the six-hour drive to get here. Can't wait to get the return jaunt home behind me. Better still, I wish the early morning journey never happened.

The word ambivalent comes to mind. Imagining myself as a duty-bound WWII bomber pilot about to unload on the civilian population of Dresden, I expect I'm feeling something approaching the level of ambivalence needed in that situation. Going through the motions; terrible motions. Bursts of dread percolate up from my gut like flack rising to discourage my self-destructive flight to shame.

No...this is wrong. I don't want to do this.

*It's my duty—just do it.*

I will hate this job.

*I need this job—live with it.*

Leave.

*No, stay on target.*

I don't want to be here.

*Shut up, and stay on target.*

This job will kill me.

*Man up! Quit being a pussy.*

Peeling back the left sleeve of my power suit jacket, and cuff-linked dress shirt, the twenty-dollar, black plastic Casio on my wrist reports 5:45 p.m. I expel air through pursed lips like a dry-rotted tire letting go. I'm stranded without a spare.

The Director of Hospital Facilities steps into the doorway, smiling. A former officer in the Army Corps of Engineers, his demeanor and body language exudes military bearing.

"Still digesting the Great White Meal?"

"Ha."

He is referring to our lunch earlier today in the hospital staff cafeteria consisting of mashed potatoes, cauliflower, and pale chicken breast.

"I was impressed. How does the chef manage to extract all of the flavor from the food?" I inquire.

"I'm afraid that is a secret. If I told you, I would have to kill you."

We both laugh.

The director is much more solid and serious than me. Standing eye-to-eye, he mirrors my close-cut hair, and well-trimmed mustache—the grayed version of myself in ten to fifteen years.

"Chuck, everyone agrees, you're our hands-down top candidate."

5

"I'm glad to hear that," I respond from the I-love-to-be-flattered quadrant of my psyche.

"I realize you would not be considering this job but for the bad economy. Whatever your reasons, I'd like for you to get the job."

"You can keep going with the glowing comments."

"Ha, I'm confident we would work well together. You'd be a real asset to me, but first...you must survive your final interview. Our Hospital Administrator maintains an iron-fisted grip on final hiring authority, and...to be blunt, he's the rudest, most difficult, and biggest...uh...well, the technical term is, asshole, I've ever known. He hates his job, and takes it out on anyone who happens to be within range."

Recalling an old western movie, I picture myself as the buck-skin-wearing frontiersman captured by hostile Indians. Bloodied, but alive, most of the gauntlet is behind me. Just one more life-or-death challenge. By defeating their greatest warrior, I will earn perquisite life-time membership in the tribe. I will marry the chief's most beautiful daughter. The ensuing communal dance will convey my Indian princess and me to our honeymoon teepee. I will grow my hair, add feathers to my wardrobe, and be given an Indian name (maybe *Stands with a List*). That notion transforms into a prison movie. I'm serving a life-sentence. Perhaps I will develop an interest in birds.

"Other than complaints left on my answering machine—in the middle of the night—he rarely speaks to me. He's seldom sighted out-side his office; when he is, what he says and does always causes a buzz among hospital staff.

"Whatever happens, whatever he says, keep your cool. Do not take offense—don't give him the satisfaction," the director says with emphasis.

I fight the urge to throw off the mantle of responsibility, escape, get as far away from where I'm standing as possible.

"With any luck, he'll hire you. Oh, be sure to kiss his ass...he expects it."

"My specialty; I hope he presents a good target."

"Don't worry about that," he says, grinning. "What possible objec-tion could he conjure?" he wonders aloud.

"Trust me, I can get along with anyone."

I recall a random discussion with a doctor who sat next to me the first few weeks of my MBA program. Before dropping out due to the demands of the curriculum, he told me the practice of placing medical doctors in charge of hospitals is misguided.

"Hospitals are big businesses. Medical doctors do not have the background to oversee big business. Truth is, good doctors practice medicine, not run hospitals. MBAs should run hospitals."

At the time, I didn't hold an opinion on the subject.

Making our way down corridors, and up elevators, anxiety builds. Intolerance for tyrants is innate to me. The submissive gene is missing from my DNA—a career limiting mutation for military officers, and as I'm discovering, for civilians as well.

Arriving at the administrator's office, I take a deep breath, and set my mind to paying homage—kissing ass. Inane visions of a shining life, free of military strictures, mock me. The director knocks, and we push into the room. A little beep from my Casio informs me it is 6:00 p.m.

Mid-sixties, disheveled, and plump, the administrator is the one thing out of place amidst the polished quality of the room. He has it all, the precise décor of my dream office, even the wall of floor-to-ceiling windows. He does not react to our entrance. Seated in a high-back reddish leather swivel-chair, he's hunched over a cherry desk in the act of reading and marking a document. Stepping to within a few paces, we await invitation to the seats on either side of us. Studying the chair closest to me, I note the tight-padded leather fashioned by a pattern of buttons and brass-tack edges on a rich cherry frame.

"Doctor, this is Charles Wilson, the candidate I am recommending as my primary assistant."

Listening as if for the impact echo of a stone dropped into a bottomless pit...nothing. Our meeting reflects from the dark beyond the massive windows to our left.

The top of the administrator's head remains aimed at us. Plowing his fingernails backward and forward across a field of shedding scalp, he tills a sparse crop of hair. Like a winter squall, flakes fall, and accumulate on the black desk-blotter below.

His head twitches as he cycles the focal point of narrow reading glasses left-right, left-right down the page. How can sight penetrate the layers of smudges, and dust on the lenses perched near the tip of his nose?

To avoid falling out of our two-man, military-like formation, I shift my weight from one leg to the other, then back as ceremonial guards are trained to do. I alternate dangling my arms at my sides, clasping my hands in front, and then behind. The administrator picks up the manuscript and swivels his chair 180 degrees, leaving us to stare at the vast backside. A picture of him stroking a hairless cat comes to mind. Reversing rotation, he returns the document to his desk, and the spectacle continues, punctuated by throat-clearing grunts.

For amusement, I play Sherlock Holmes analyzing the room with minimal head movement. Eye-drying vapor of a recently used cleaning chemical is in the air. The administrator's shirt and tie are soiled and wrinkled—the obvious combination of lunch and a nap. The remains of a meal lay in a roadkill-like heap at the edge of his desk. Fresh from a nap, his face retains the corduroy imprint of a pillow stuffed against one arm of the couch to my right. Absurd meanings for "M.D.," the letters etched into his nameplate following his name, spark in my mind: Mad Dander, Maximus Dandruffus, Mister Dumpy?

My game of deductions ends when the administrator slams his head-scratching hand flat onto the manuscript in front of him. Imagining a fallout cloud of displaced epidermis drifting my way, I hold my breath. Should I duck and cover, as in a nuclear attack? Abandoning the code of propriety keeping me from looking at what he is editing, I recognize the ivory linen watermarked paper—with matching envelopes—I invested top-dollar in at the print shop. My stomach constricts as he scrawls *BS!!!* in the 1.25-inch margin of my resume. Face burning, the scrape of his high-end fountain pen causes an angry swell of blood to pump into my brain.

Like an abused child, I suffer silently. *Stand down, remain calm,* I coax, and recall a limerick-like mantra coached by my headhunter:

"The goal of a job *interview* is to get a job *offer.* Then decide whether *you* want the *job.*"

The concept had seemed so simple.

Feeling violated, and breathing rage, I shift into high-gear, second-guessing every decision leading me to this alien city. Stuck, powerless, suspended like a spider's next meal— bitterness overwhelms my senses.

Grasping for balance—a happy place —I recall a moment of good feelings I experienced the previous month. Following a longed-for third interview with a major bank, the Senior Vice President walks me out of his bright, modern, black leather, and chrome corner office, complete with floor-to-ceiling windows. His arm is draped across my shoulders as if I'm his son or he is a coach and I'm his favorite player. More like a conversation with a close uncle than a job interview, there is a delicious center of informality within the fresh-pressed power suits and formal trappings. I've made it, I think.

Smiling and shaking my hand, the Senior Vice President says, "Chuck, I see great things for you. We will be in touch with a job offer within a few days. I hope we can convince you to come to work for us. You are a good fit for our organization."

Ah, I like the tailored feel of the term *good fit.* At last, my efforts and judgment are vindicated—validated. Leaving the Navy was a good idea after all. I am weightless, walking on air.

Departing the shining building of glass and marble, I swoop down to thank the secretary responsible for coordinating the interview.

Looking up, she asks, "Did you hear about the stock market crash? They're saying it's the worst day ever on Wall Street."

The day was the seventh of October 1987—still referred to as Black Friday.

After a week of incessant inquiries, I am informed by an Assistant Vice President, "Mr. Wilson, I'm sorry to inform you, but due to the

9

recent financial meltdown, our bank's board of directors has imposed a hiring freeze. If you are still available when this economic storm blows over—perhaps in the spring—please contact us."

"Meltdown, freeze, storm." Catastrophes always draw competing metaphors. A thanks-but-no-thanks letter soon followed.

Similar confused metaphors are offered by my other hot job prospects—if they return my repeated calls. Hope of ever reaching the shores of the *me* I had set out for fades.

Wishing for the skill to desire jobs I do not want is perplexing. Reality can suck.

"Well, sit down—that's what those chairs are there for," I am jostled out of my thoughts by the administrator, who scoffs upon taking notice of us.

Without the courtesy of a handshake, or allowing us time to get fully seated, he assails, "I see nothing in this," tapping my resume with a too-long index fingernail, "that makes me want to hire you. In fact, it tells me the opposite."

Stunned—completely off kilter—I struggle to formulate a response. My body stiffens for battle.

"Mr. Wilson, your being here, interviewing for this job, makes no sense. Your resume betrays a life of unrelated experiences. Your bachelor's degree is in English with an emphasis in writing. So, what in hell did you intend to become with that major, Assistant Director of Facilities at this hospital? I don't think so."

Divining my life as if from tea leaf residue on the page, his voice reflects a rising level of irritation.

"Let's see, your first job out of college was selling advertising and writing movie reviews for a newspaper. You lasted six months doing that. Then, you put your college degree to work peddling life insurance. What was that like: knocking on doors, calling people during their dinner, talking insurance at every cocktail party you could get invited to, pushing expensive whole-life policies to your friends and relatives so you could pay your bills?"

Somehow, he sure knows a lot about selling insurance. He continues wrapping me in his web.

"You worked hard, and won several sales awards: Agent of the Quarter three times, you set a company record for new agent sales, but you hated every minute, didn't you? After one year, you couldn't take it anymore. To escape, to exit stage-right, you joined the Navy. Another lifelong dream, I'm sure.

"Hmm, Officer Candidate School, various other Navy schools; you spent four years on a ship, did a few other great things nobody cares about, blah blah blah. Then you landed an assignment at the University of Rochester where you spent the last few years playing professor for the Navy ROTC. In your spare time, you completed a Master's Degree in Business Administration at—as you describe here—one of the top twenty-five business schools in the country. The all-powerful MBA we hear so much about these days. Big deal!

"Mr. Wilson, you remind me of a hot-air balloon, floating through life without a plan."

He pauses to assess the damage he's done. From the look on my face, he knows his analysis is balls-on accurate. I can barely wiggle. Maintaining eye contact, he dials his mouth into a twisted smile.

"But, winter is here. Cold hard reality is setting in. You're out of the Navy. Off the dole. The economy's in the toilet. MBAs are now a dime-a-dozen, and the winds have blown you here—to *my* office—to bother *me* for a job, and piss *me* off!

"Mr. Wilson, I don't need you, with your M-B-A, and Bachelor of Arts degree, to be my Assistant Director of Facilities. I want someone built from the ground up for *that* job—not *mine*."

He shifts his scowl back to my resume.

"Right here," he says, scoring an already underlined section, "you could not resist mentioning 'writing' under hobbies. I love it when people list their hobbies—it's so revealing. I have no desire to employ a wannabe writer except, perhaps, to assist with my memoirs someday. The worst thing I could do for either of us is hire you. One year from now you'll be frustrated because I will not agree to pay you enough to keep you interested. You'll be miserable, and looking for somewhere else to work. Someplace new to waste your life for a few years. Then, your accomplice there," he points at the director, "will be disturbing me with another character from his fantasy island of ex-military misfits."

M.D. shifts his view, and growls at the director, "If you had provided this resume to me in advance—as I require—we would not be putting ourselves through this. I will not be manipulated into a bad hire. I should not have agreed to this meeting."

Turning back to me, he says, "Mr. Wilson, I don't care what you do when you leave this office, but here's some free advice, take it for what it's worth…figure out what the hell you want in life, and pursue it. Quit wandering the earth chasing paychecks!"

Truth is not polite company.

Despising M.D. for his insights, it hits me—this self-loathing creature, reeking of regret, is a possible future me. What choice do I have? Anger rises as the unsound foundation of my fabricated identity crumbles; as the facade veiling legions of self-deceits is razed. I am naked, juvenile, and false—unprepared and inadequate to bear exposure of the real me—especially to myself.

I start to speak, to defend my life, but I don't get a chance. Like a cop stopping traffic, he flashes a flat palm.

The sour look on his face twists into a sneer, "Besides, your experience on a ship in no way qualifies you for this job. You don't know how to manage the facilities of this hospital."

Fighting to ignore the growing realization I could somehow become like him, I scramble for footing amongst the rubble of my life, finding traction on the grounds that I need employment—self-fulfilling or not. His otherwise brilliant assault has a flaw. He is wrong about one thing—I know how to manage his facilities.

"Sir, I spent much of my time, as a naval officer, in charge of the operation and repair of facilities on a ship that are even more complex than those that support this building. I was responsible for electrical distribution, plumbing, power generation, air-conditioning, steam heating, etc., as well as casualty response, safety programs, fire prevention, painting, and preservation. I know how to solve big problems, and lead teams of technicians conducting repairs, troubleshooting, and performing routine maintenance—simultaneously!"

His eyes narrow as he rejoins the melee.

"You're a smart guy, but a few years on a ship do not qualify you for this job. You know nothing about building construction," he taunts.

The director had mentioned plans to expand the hospital during our talks.

"Sir, a ship is a building—except it also has to go to sea. I may have been an English/Writing Arts major as an undergrad, but I grew up working construction. My father was a contractor, and I worked for him, from the age of twelve, building houses from the ground up. I can do it all: masonry, carpentry, electrical, plumbing."

"Finally, you've said something of value to me. Why doesn't your resume mention your construction background? Obviously, it wasn't written with a job like this in mind."

He enjoys deducing answers to his own questions. Looking at me for a long moment, he rubs his neck and chin like a savvy horse-trader considering the qualities of an animal.

Quivering with adrenaline, I'm kicking myself for having removed the years of construction experience from my resume. I begin to once more defend my qualifications, but again, his palm stops me. He pauses for a second; looks me up and down. I perceive he is weighing this new information against his previous assessment of me. A negative side-to-side shake of his head makes his decision clear.

"You'd be gone within a year."

He dismisses us with a backhanded shoofly wave.

Standing, I reach out to shake his hand. Ignoring me, he lifts the receiver of his telephone, and begins to dial. A tug at my sleeve by the director breaks the spell.

"Send housekeeping to my office," I hear as we depart the room.

The weight of the world is on my shoulders—not a fatherly arm.

A safe distance away, the director speaks from somewhere next to me, "Forgot to mention, he's a germaphobe as well as an asshole."

Looking at the director with what must be wild eyes, a suppressed laugh rocks my aching lungs.

Crossing Pennsylvania on my drive home, agitation grows. The scene in the administrator's office replays again and again. Memories bubble up. I recall getting married between my second and third years of college. After graduation, I earned less at the newspaper with a college degree than as frozen foods manager at ACME Markets, a job I worked while still in high school—another job that didn't make its way into my resume.

Glowering at the dark road ahead, I shout at the heavens, demand justice from God—an entity in whose existence I do not believe. I'm a devout agnostic, for God's sake. Mile-by-mile I catalogue my grievances.

Stupid headhunter. Why did he send me there? What a waste.

My hero/hunter complex aches with shame. I am returning home with no prize despite saint-worthy acts.

Stupid administrator. Could he not see the obvious glow about me?

I resent responsibility, and groveling for a job I do not want in a place I have no desire to live. I can't believe a position as basic as Assistant Director of Facilities is a brass-ring beyond my grasp on the carousel of life.

Doesn't my willingness to sacrifice my dreams count for something?

Avoiding the depths, I seek solace in the shallows of consolation. That hospital does not deserve me. That job is beneath me.

My route across Pennsylvania includes a long stretch of road that should long have been a four-lane divided highway. Winding my way up an eternal incline, held back by an incommodious procession of tractor trailers, I am overcome by a sense of suffocation.

Pennsylvania, your roads suck!

Desperate for air, for progress of some kind, I pull into the oncoming lane, and stomp the accelerator to make the grade. The two-lane highway arcs upward to the right. The headlights of a fast-approaching vehicle appear with less than a truck-length separating us. I am about to be dead. There is no time, nowhere to go. My remains will be indistinguishable from those in the oncoming vehicle sharing my vanishing point. Face-to-face with certain collision, tucked within a razor-thin instant in time, an impossible opening just large enough for my four-cylinder hatchback appears to my right. Like a child fleeing a nightmare for the snug space between sleeping parents, I dive in. Disapproving high beams from the truck, a whisker from my rear window, illuminate the interior of my car like the inside of a lightbulb.

Ignoring the undeserved miracle of still being alive, I rage at the unfairness of life, hammer the dash, ceiling, and steering wheel with ungrateful fists. To escape the judgment of the fuming trucker at my bumper, I chance an edging glance up the dark highway, yank left into the passing lane, and scream into the night, squeezing everything I can out of my 1980 Plymouth Champ.

Exhausted, and broken, I arrive at our country home west of Rochester in Holley, New York. Making my way through the house in the dark, I feel like a ghost—an apparition. Not here. From the open door of the bedroom where my sons sleep, I ponder their beauty in the soft glow of a Spiderman nightlight. Both are wearing their Superman pajamas. Do they consider me a superhero?

The light from my bedside clock glows 2:00 a.m., illuminating my entry between the cool bed covers. It has been twenty-four hours to the minute since that timepiece caused me to begin my day. As if joining a campfire, I stop at the just-right edge of my wife's radiating warmth. Lying on my back, too tense to enjoy the comfort of my pillow, I remove and fold my thick glasses, and imagine the day has not happened; that I never left.

I'm not going to set that damn alarm. I'm going to sleep until naturally I wake up.

"How did it go?" Debbie asks from near-sleep.

"Fine," I lie.

"Did you get a job offer?"

"Not yet. I'll tell you all about it in the morning," I say, too tired and too ashamed to provide an honest answer.

"I'm so glad you're home. I can't sleep when you're away. I have to get up at five...teaching first thing in the morning."

She is in the final weeks of completing her student-teaching requirement. The last thing needed to earn her teaching credential.

"You had better get to sleep, babe."

"I was thinking about when we first met."

She loves to reminisce.

"I've always wondered what caused you to sit down beside me?"

"I liked your smile," she replies.

It's 1974. With ten cold snowmobile riding and bumper-jumping days of early January left as a sixteen-year-old, I am a junior in high school when Debbie and I meet. She is ten months older, nearly eighteen, and a senior. Great smile or not, it is a good thing she is not initially aware of this age disparity. Bumper-jumping, by the way, is the practice of hiding in bushes near a stop sign on nights when the streets are covered with snow. The goal is to grab hold of the rear bumper of stopping cars, unseen, and then be pulled in a crouched position with your boots as skis, over as much of the town as possible.

A close friend, Mike Schuschereba, is working at ACME Market after school, and one of his co-workers is having a party at his parents' house in Bath. Mike has taken the liberty of inviting me and a few other friends from our hometown of Avoca to attend. We all ride together in what we refer to as *The Van*. Technically, *The Van* belongs to my friend

Kris Goodrich, but the sense of ownership has been diluted with sweat equity. Because of our many hours of work, we consider it *our* van. Deep blue, it has wide-ass tires, a bed in the back, four captain's chairs, and shag carpet floor to ceiling. A nightmare to fathers of daughters between ages sixteen and eighteen. If you see this van a-rocking, don't come a-knocking.

The party house is packed tight with people. Most are wearing heavy winter wear. The majority are high school seniors who have recently or are about to turn eighteen—the legal drinking age. Other than my fellow Avocans—Kris, Bruce, and Mike—I know no one at the party. Swimming through the crowd, I edge past a guy with shoulder-length hair dumping beer into a fish-tank and laughing. In reaction, a variety of tropical fish school to the fluid being introduced. Would hate for someone to do that to my fish. *Should I say something?* I don't.

A fistful of ski passes hanging from the zipper of my coat emote cool. The same adornment identifies several fellow skiers scattered throughout the crowd. A few passes hang from actual ski jackets. The wearers must have rich parents.

It's an old house with low ceilings, and the floor is alive, moving up and down with the waves of energy passing through the crowd. We cross the shag carpet in the dining room, and make it to the linoleum floor in the kitchen. It is slick with snowmelt. The smell of beer permeates. Noticing the breakfast nook is unoccupied, we slide in, two per side. Kris in the back corner, and Mike next to him across from me. Bruce is against the wall to my left. We are all skinny wrestlers, so there is room for company. A guy Mike knows sits down next to him, and begins conversation.

Our visitor notices the containers of basil, parmesan, and red pepper poised at the end of the table awaiting family pizza-night.

"Hey, man, I have an idea," he says.

He pulls a pack of Zig-Zag cigarette papers out of his coat pocket, licks and joins two of the tiny translucent squares together to make an extra wide surface, and rolls up a mix of the spices. The finished product looks like the cigarettes my hillbilly great-uncles roll day-in and day-out with Prince Albert tobacco. Prince Albert tobacco tins, sized to fit in your back pocket, are perfect for reuse, storing a day's supply of night crawlers when fishing.

Like a fish lured from murky depths to the near surface, an eager face appears from the crowd lapping at our table. It's the guy who had been serving beer to the citizenry of the aquarium.

"Hey, man, are you goin' tuh smoke that?"

"No, man, you want it?" Mike's friend says, and offers up his product.

"Yeah! Cool!"

The bait is snatched. The happy face rolls away, and is gone from sight.

"Shouldn't we stop him?" I ask.

"Why do you think they call it dope, man?" Mike's friend says with a grin, parroting an anti-drug commercial.

We all laugh. A bit uncomfortable with the transaction, I have an inkling something less than grand will soon result. Any thoughts of chasing the guy down and stopping what's about to take place are scattered when a pretty girl surfaces, and strikes up a conversation with us.

"So, where are you guys from?" she asks.

"Avoca," I reply.

"You look just like a guy I know, from Prattsburg," she says, pointing at my companion, Bruce, to my left.

"I hear that all of the time. I'm Bruce Sager."

She slides in close beside me. Leaning back to allow her to talk past me with Bruce, I lose myself in the sight of her long brown hair just under my chin. The most perfect scent I have ever inhaled takes up residence in my nostrils and brain. Turning her face toward me, brown eyes shining like mercury dimes, she smiles. My heart stops. I can't breathe.

"I'm Debbie Pruden, what's your name?"

"Uh...I'm...Chuck Wilson. Uh...everybody calls me Farkle."

"Farkle? Like on *Laugh-In*?"

"Yeah."

Some angry individual broaches at the head of the table.

"You guys are assholes. My friend almost died smoking that shit you gave him."

Mike's friend, the culprit, has disappeared. Ignoring the explanations being given by my friends, I focus on talking to Debbie.

"You must like to ski," she says, pointing at my bundle of ski passes.

"I love it."

"Me too."

"We should go skiing together, sometime," I say.

Can't believe I just said that. I'm in way over my head.

"Okay, but I have to break up with my boyfriend, first."

"Okay."

Ten minutes later she informs me she has, in fact, broken up with her boyfriend. Our life together begins.

Dead-awake, eyes clenched shut, the oncoming headlights are branded into memory. A battle rages between fear of death and a secret desire for the release it offers. The forces of close-call thankfulness are outgunned by putrid resentment.

I'm worthless...worthless. Why do I even exist? Is there a final judgment? I don't care anymore. Things can't be any worse. I wish I were dead.

Sometime in the night, dismissing the grace of the impossible gap in traffic as coincidence, I find peace in the wreckage. Memory of that pivotal sliver of time, poised between my vanishing point and survival without a scratch, imbeds itself in my psychological skin to fester and render meaning for decades.

I'm anchored deep in a dark dreamless sleep until I hear Debbie's voice, "Chuck! Chuck! Wake up! Wake up!"

*Thud.* I feel knees slam into me. Water drops, from wet hair, rain on my face.

"Feel...there's a lump! Found it while taking my shower."

# CHAPTER 2

# THE LUMP

*(Debbie)*

Damn. It's 5:00 a.m. Reaching out from under the covers, I find the alarm, shut it off, and force myself out of bed. Eyes barely open, I shuffle to the bathroom. Chuck arrived home a few hours ago from a job interview in a distant city. He didn't say so, but I don't think things went well. I know it's bad news when he won't say anything. Nothing new, things have not been going well for a while.

In one month, I will complete a semester of student-teaching, the final leg in my ten-year voyage to become a certified teacher. As a Navy wife, I have navigated a series of colleges—a semester here, a year of classes there—between military moves and the births of two sons. The oldest, Brian, is now in second grade. Greg just turned four. My days are chockablock, beginning crazy early. Work on the next day's lesson plans begins only after both boys are in bed asleep, and ends when exhaustion pours over me like rising floodwaters overwhelming a sandbag fortress.

The science lesson I'm presenting this morning has me worried. Science is my most challenging subject. Even teaching fifth graders, I feel compelled to know everything. That raises my stress level. I'm not sure I'm cut out to be a teacher.

Stepping into the shower, I let the hot water rain down my body for a long moment to wake me up before reaching for the body wash. My hands glide on the slick, soapy film. Adrenaline surges the instant my fingers discover a firm, marble-sized bump in my left breast. I'm thirty-one years old, and wide-awake.

My brain is in high gear. I have never been more frantic.

"Chuck...

"I need to see my doctor right away. I don't understand—I just had an appointment two months ago...he did a thorough breast exam!"

My breathing is shallow, driven with panic.

"What if it's cancer? It can't be cancer, not now! I can't die—who will raise my boys?

"What about my students? My mentor-teachers are counting on me to be there, today. I'm supposed to instruct all morning classes. Can't do it. Need to call them. I need to call the school!"

Contacting my mentor-teachers at home, I wake them up. It's only 5:15 a.m., but they are sympathetic. The person manning the phone at the elementary school in Brockport tells me to do whatever I need to do to take care of myself.

Tears flowing, my fingers continue to explore the lump, expecting it will suddenly not be there; hoping I somehow made a mistake.

"I think I'm making it worse!"

Chuck holds me tight as I sob, quake, and gasp for breath.

Struggling to formulate a measured response to a life-altering discovery, questions boil over.

"What does this mean?

"How will this affect our plans?

"How can this be happening? The timing couldn't be worse!

"How can God let this happen? This isn't fair!"

Our world is spinning out of control.

With hours to go before I can possibly speak to someone at my gynecologist's office, I'm occupying my mind with routine tasks like getting Brian ready for school, and Greg to his babysitter. Activity is precious to mental health during a crisis: feed, wash, dress, provide lunch money, sign the permission slip for the field trip to Eastman KODAK, aim Brian out the door to catch the school bus at the end of our long driveway. Greg does not want to go to his babysitter. He never does.

"I want to stay home, and play with my toys," he demands.

"You may take a few of your toys with you," I bribe.

"I want to play with them here," he insists.

"You can either choose a few toys to take with you or you can go without," I say, playing hardball.

Unhappy, he chooses a couple of favorites. After a few more skirmishes, Chuck loads him in our car, and off they go. His current sitter is a very patient and kind lady with a magic touch, who lives a mile away. A challenging child, a previous sitter requested we make other childcare arrangements. Greg had crossed the threshold of one bite too many on her children. She suggested a muzzle.

At 7:30 a.m., I begin dialing my doctor's office number every ten minutes.

"This isn't fair. This isn't fair."

Chuck attempts to reassure me.

"Debbie, everything is going to be okay."

"Are you sure?"

"Yes."

He knows better than to express doubt.

I can't help but feel angry. These past two years have been a pressure cooker. While raising two young sons—and performing extensive improvements to a fixer-upper house situated on seven acres with an in-ground pool and horse barn—I completed my bachelor's degree in Elementary Education in May. Normally, the student-teaching requirement is completed before graduating, but during my travels, I accumulated many extra semester hours of college credit that did nothing to move me along the required course track. So, when I finally crossed all those essentials off the list, I opted to graduate. I had waited long enough for that diploma. My 3.97 GPA—all As, but for one B (in Motivational

Theory!)—gives me great pride and a sense of accomplishment. Also, Chuck completed an MBA program, and against my wishes, left the Navy expecting to find big-money in the corporate world.

At 9:00 a.m., the receptionist answers the phone at my gynecologist's office.

"Sorry, Mrs. Wilson, but there are no appointments available until next Tuesday."

Unwilling to take no for an answer, I ask to speak to the nurse. She listens to my situation, and agrees to squeeze me in around 11:00 a.m. We arrive an hour early.

Upon examination, Dr. Robischon assures me the lump is nothing to worry about.

"You're only thirty-one years old, and very healthy. It's extremely unlikely you have breast cancer. I'm certain it's a cyst, but to put your mind at ease, I'll arrange for a needle aspiration."

It so happens that the nearby surgeon he recommends has an immediate opening. Chuck and I walk to Dr. Penn's office on an anti-treasure hunt, searching hard for something we do not want to find.

Dr. Penn informs us the lump is almost certainly a cyst, and will collapse as the fluid is drawn off by the needle. Praying this scare has a happy ending, I look forward to driving home while feeling silly for overreacting. Lying on an examination table, I watch the point of the large needle first indent, then pierce, my skin and slide under measured pressure into position at the core of the marble-sized mass. With steady skill, Dr. Penn pulls the needle plunger to create suction. Focusing on the clear glass chamber, I wait for some disgusting fluid to flow, and "The Lump" to collapse. Nothing happens. A slight look of surprise appears on the surgeon's face.

"Why isn't anything coming out?" I ask as fear resurges.

"No need for concern. All is well," Dr. Penn counters. "There are plenty of benign explanations for this mass. I will need to perform an excisional biopsy, but that procedure is a little more complex. I will need to bring you back in a few days. I have a room here in my office where I perform minor surgery."

Two days later, I am back in Dr. Penn's waiting room. Nancy, my little sister, is with me. She is as scared as I am. Seven years younger, her bright brown eyes beam unconditional love and support.

"Debbie, I know everything is going to be fine. I'm not going to let anything happen to my big sister," she says when a nurse calls my name to take me back.

Dr. Penn allows Chuck to be with me during the procedure. Chuck holds my hand as Dr. Penn hides his work from our view with a short blue surgical curtain, and distracts us with questions and personal stories. He numbs the area with a local anesthetic, administered with a small needle, so some tugging is all I feel during the surgery.

"Can I see it?" I ask.

Dr. Penn pulls back a blue cloth covering a stainless steel tray. There it is: the lump. I stare at the oblong, brownish nodule covered with beads of white fatty-looking material.

"Tastes like chicken," he jokes. "It will take a few days for the lab to verify exactly what it is, but it does not appear cancerous to me. I will contact you immediately in the unlikely event the pathology results are of concern."

We drive home, struggling to be hopeful.

In the meantime, I'm keeping myself busy with classroom responsibilities. A perfectionist, I always arrive in the classroom well before my mentor-teachers. Ten years older, and much more committed than the average student-teacher, I fret overlooked details in lesson plans, and fear being unable to answer possible questions posed by sixth graders. Can't stop prepping until I know everything.

Chuck and I enjoy visualizing our future: my teacher salary pooled with the income from his "big money" job, and the nice house, vacations, and lifestyle. Stress and doubt mount as the duration of his unemployment extends, and our savings dwindle.

Anticipating a location change, we agreed to sell our house last month. The sale is scheduled to close in less than two weeks. Next week movers will arrive to pack and carry our household goods to storage. Our plan is to stay for about a month with local friends until I finish student-teaching. Eventually, if a job does not materialize for Chuck, we will migrate to a small upstairs apartment at his grandmother's farmhouse. Perhaps I will have the opportunity to work as a substitute teacher at Chuck's old elementary school in Watkins Glen. At Grandma's, we can live cheaply until our reemergence into the world. We have it all figured out. Everything is under control.

For now, my good friend and fellow student-teacher, Marsha Crosier, is insisting we move into their home for the remaining weeks of the semester. Marsha hatched the plan with the support of her husband, Nelson. Chuck and I are astonished by the generosity of their offer. It's exactly what we need, although at first, we did not feel comfortable imposing on them—especially with two very active children. We always feel we must handle whatever life throws at us on our own.

"Debbie, we have plenty of room in our house. Chuck can continue his search for a job; Brian can remain with his second-grade class until Christmas break, and Greg gets to spend his days with a familiar babysitter. It's the perfect solution. Come on, it'll be fun!"

"I'm going to remind you of saying that," I say.

"Okay, I hope we are still friends after you have us around your house for a month."

### (Chuck)

Debbie is having her stitches removed today. She insisted I remain home, working my way down her list of last minute projects. The packers arrive tomorrow. Household moves are a lot of work, even when professionals are doing the lion's share. It's mid-morning. The phone rings—it's Dr. Penn. A red dawn is breaking.

"Mr. Wilson, I thought for sure you would be coming to my office today with your wife. I'm so sorry to tell you like this, but the biopsy report is not what we had hoped. The lump tested positive for infiltrating inter-ductal breast cancer."

"No!" I exhale as if punched in the stomach.

"Can you get here right away? I haven't told your wife yet, she's sitting in my personal office waiting for me. I'm sorry...I really expected you would be here with her. Should I wait for you to arrive before...?"

In shock, I struggle to answer a question that requires clear thinking.

"No...go ahead...tell her," I say. "I'm an hour away. She'll figure it out long before I get there."

Hanging up the phone, I am stunned, scarcely able to function.

"My wife has cancer...I can't go there wearing these dirty work clothes...how do I change?"

I wander through the house in a fog.

"Shoes...I need shoes. I haven't shaved. Should I shower?"

Somehow, I get myself ready and drive to Rochester. Upon arrival, I am ushered to Dr. Penn's office. Debbie is there, seated next to a nurse. Her face is red, and wet, a Kleenex box in her lap—wads of clenched tissues. Our eyes connect. Sobbing, she rises into my arms, and melts. Fighting to detach from the emotions, I maintain decorum.

Once home, Debbie begins contacting her parents and sister to tell them about the cancer. Tough conversations. Lots of tears. She heads to bed. Doubt she will find any sleep. Time to inform my family.

"Grandma, Debbie has...cuh...she has...cuh...cuh-cancer."

The word "cancer" catches in my throat like a wrench dropped into a running engine. Breaking down, I cry for the first time since my childhood. It hurts like hell.

A feeling of other-worldliness hangs over me in the coming days. It's as if my hands and feet belong to someone else operating them by remote control. A team of movers arrive, and spend two days packing, and loading our belongings onto a van for transfer to long-term storage. Standing on our front porch, we watch as the massive tractor trailer makes its way out of our long driveway.

"I feel as empty as our house," Debbie says. "How long will it be before we see our stuff again?"

"Everything's going to be okay, babe."

Surgery to widen the margins around the original tumor site, and remove several lymph nodes (to determine whether the cancer has spread), takes place the day before Thanksgiving. My in-laws join me for Thanksgiving dinner in the Genesee Hospital cafeteria. Another flavorless "great-white-meal."

We are adrift.

### *(Debbie)*

It's Friday, the day after Thanksgiving, when we return to the Crozier's home. My intention is to return to the classroom by Wednesday, having missed only a few days. After listening to me feel sorry for myself, Marsha, against my stated wishes, contacts the minister of a small local Methodist church we attend occasionally.

It is Sunday, late in the afternoon, when the minister comes for a visit. Chuck, not wanting anything to do with the meeting, sequesters himself in our upstairs bedroom.

As the minister and I speak, the early dark of the season fills our friends' living room with shadows. Among their furniture and mementos, I release a torrent of confused thoughts and emotions.

Through tears I tell the pastor, "I don't deserve God's love...God is punishing me for not coming to church...God is unfair—cancer should only happen to people much worse than me."

He takes my hands in his, looks me in the eyes, and tells me, "God loves his children, and does not want us to suffer. You are not being punished. People are diagnosed with cancer every day. Sickness happens in this world, even to the kindest, best, most devout of Christians. After all, he allowed his own son to die, and he was innocent. God will give you the strength to get through this, and somehow, God will bring good out of this terrible situation."

Part of me does not buy what he is selling, but what I hear rings together true with a sleeping inner-knowledge. We pray together. The combination of tumbling circumstances aligns, cracking the door open to my heart and mind. Light seeps into my soul, feeding my dormant faith. I step past the superstitions and misunderstandings comprising my belief system, one by one.

The next morning, I am informed the remaining few weeks of my student teaching have been waived. Citing my work ethic, maturity, and demonstrated skills, they say I'm more than ready to be a classroom teacher. This means we can shorten our imposition on our friends, the Croziers. So many people are doing wonderful things for us. Maybe things will be okay.

# CHAPTER 3

# TO GRANDMOTHER'S HOUSE WE GO

### *(Chuck)*

We move to the apartment over my grandmother's house in early December—my first home as a child. Growing up, my grandmother was the most dependable and influential person in my life. As her oldest grandchild, our relationship runs deep. Grandma's farm is a place of safety, always available during transitional periods in my life. Located within earshot of Watkins Glen International, the whine of high performance racecars wafting down from the hilltop speedway is the background soundtrack to my earliest memories.

Just before Christmas, a sheriff's deputy knocks on our door. Debbie and I are being sued for $50,000—a sum beyond our comprehension—by a man whose purchase offer we had turned down (for our former house in Holley, New York). This man showed up unannounced, with his proposal—insisting we sign right away or he would buy a different house. Our real estate agent was out of town. His bid was contingent upon several things, including the sale of *his* home. Hesitant to agree to the sale without our realtor's advice, but afraid to look a gift-horse in the mouth, we accepted the deal conditionally—contingent upon our attorney's final approval. A few days later, our attorney advised we decline the man's proposal and, instead, accept a much better contract from a different buyer. Two years of hard work had turned our fixer-upper into a desirable property. That should be a good thing, right?

Damn, a lawsuit. One more thing heaped on our already-full plate of things to be angry about. Our real estate attorney informs us he does not do litigation. Further, he holds no responsibility for our being sued even though we acted on his advice. He recommends another attorney. Our meager supply of cash is evaporating.

The ninety-day health insurance policy we bought when I left the Navy runs out at the end of December. In January, I discover I am entitled to thirteen weeks of unemployment benefits. Assuming that leaving the Navy of my own accord makes me ineligible, I did not bother to apply—wrong, again. Debbie cannot resist pointing out that the extra money would have been helpful. I can't blame her. One more thing to feel stupid about. That plate is full too.

My failings as a husband and father fill my thoughts. The only wise thing I have done is join the Navy Reserve. At least I have two days of work each month. During drill weekend, the Commanding Officer of the Navy Reserve Center in Rochester, Lieutenant "Buzz" Little, listens to my plight and encourages me to return to the Navy, full-time, in the TAR community—short for Training and Administration of Reserves.

"You should be a TAHHH, Chuck," Buzz promotes with a big salesman smile.

His gravelly voice, and unique pronunciation of "TAR" resonates in my thoughts on my drive home. Reluctant, but reconciled, I decide to return to my previous career path as a Surface Warfare Officer, except my future shore tours will be spent performing Navy Reserve related support duties.

Debbie is ecstatic. She loves the military lifestyle: friendships, steady paycheck, and opportunities to live in a variety of locations. Also, she believes much more than I do in my capacity to be a good naval officer.

Memories from my first sea tour haunt me. For a time, while serving on my first ship with fellow officers I enjoyed and respected, I was enthusiastic about my Navy career. Then, under a different commanding officer, my attitude turned sour. The passion I once felt was gone.

Truth is...I was scared stiff. Avoiding failure was a major factor in my motivation to leave active-duty Navy; convinced I could not motivate myself through the required schools or job of chief engineer. Ability was not the problem; without desire, I had lost steerageway. Dreading the years of stress and family separation like dirt pouring into my grave, I drifted into more anxiety than I ever imagined possible.

Because Buzz Little pollinated a thought in my brain, fear overcame fear. A mutation of desire took form. In February of 1988, after four-plus months of unemployed hell, I am welcomed back to the Navy full-time. Unknown to me, there were over two hundred applicants vying for three openings in the TAR program. The strength of my record won a battle I did not know was going on. Ignorance is bliss, sometimes.

### *(Debbie)*

While staying at Grandma's house, I undergo six weeks of daily outpatient radiation therapy, culminating in a few extra-strong electron boost treatments at a cancer center in Rochester. The sight of "CANCER" in big letters on the side of the building causes me to shudder every time.

It's February of 1988, and paychecks from the Navy have started again. Breathing without a lump of worry in my throat is now possible. Chuck says next time, they'll have to throw him out of the Navy, kicking and screaming.

Returning to life as the wife of a naval officer is a dream come true. Chuck will report to Surface Warfare Officer Department Head School in Newport, Rhode Island in August. Newport is one of my favorite towns. In the interim, he is serving as Executive Officer at the Navy and

Marine Corps Reserve Center in Rochester. The boys and I continue to live with Grandma. During the week, Chuck stays near Rochester with my cousin, Kathy Denning, and commutes to the farm on weekends. Back in the Navy family, we have health insurance, a decent income, and opportunities to experience life in new places. Security, I love security.

Believing we have elbowed our way past the breast cancer nightmare, a follow-up appointment with Dr. Penn results in a referral to an oncologist. The oncologist informs me recent studies recommend what he calls "adjuvant chemotherapy" as insurance against a recurrence of breast cancer.

Chemotherapy?

No, I'm done with cancer.

In truth, my greatest fear is losing my hair. After much angst, a close examination of the study's findings, and encouragement to do so from Chuck and others, I agree to the six-month regimen. The first thing I'm going to do is buy a wig.

After a few treatments, pain in my lower back—the same as I experienced during my pregnancy with Greg—grows extreme. The oncologist decides its cause is a urinary tract infection. He prescribes antibiotics, grants me a reprieve from the week's chemotherapy session, and switches one of the chemo drugs for another, which will impact my kidneys less. Maximum doses of ibuprofen control the incessant ache.

It's August, and we have moved to Newport. There is no oncologist assigned to the naval hospital so I'm continuing my chemotherapy treatments with an expensive civilian doctor here in town.

My back pain continues.

During an office visit, I ask the young oncologist, "Is there any possibility that cancer has spread to my kidney?"

"Mrs. Wilson, you're what we refer to as 'carcinoma-phobic.' Breast cancer simply does not metastasize to the kidneys. You're doing fine.

Focus on the future," he patronizes, dismissing my concerns with a shoofly wave.

Feeling like a child who has been ridiculed—talked down to by an impatient and infinitely superior adult—I am sick and angry. It's a tough pill from a man with so little life experience. Swallowing my fury, I know deep down, carcinoma-phobic or not, something is seriously wrong with me.

Another point of contention with this doctor: he refuses to accept anything less than what he considers full restitution for my medical bills. The amounts covered by CHAMPUS (our military dependent medical insurance) and our scheduled co-pays leave a large unpaid balance. Questioning the oncologist's bookkeeper regarding the exorbitance of his fees, I receive a snippy response echoing the character of his leadership.

"You should be thankful for being accepted as a patient. After all, the doctor's business model is focused on serving the residents of Newport. He is one of only a few oncologists on the island, and the only one willing to consider time-payment plans from military dependents."

"Business model?" He must have picked that term up at some medical practice seminar he attended. "Residents" refers to Newport's wealthy. The disgust with which the bookkeeper says "time-payment plan" makes my lowly position clear.

"Is there any way I can get some relief on the cost of my treatments?" I ask the doctor.

"Mrs. Wilson, you are always welcome to travel to Providence to seek care. I will be happy to refer you," he replies, holding firm to his business model with a programmed response.

It's clear, I'm scum; nothing to this child-like doctor. Thoughts of driving home from Providence following chemo-treatments makes my position clear. Stuck, I continue my care with him. Chuck says not to worry. Monthly payments will continue for years.

Celebrating my final treatment, I turn again toward my dream of becoming a teacher.

Surprise! My hair thinned, but remains mostly in place with a ladder of color changes indicating the timing of chemo-treatments like tree rings reveal seasons survived. Our timing does not support teaching at a public school, so I accept a position at a nearby preschool as a Toddler Teacher. The pay isn't great, but the job includes free tuition for Greg.

Teaching preschool is strenuous. Lots of lifting, setting up and putting away cots for nap time, mopping floors, and cleaning bathrooms. The worst part is wrestling kids in and out of snowsuits during the winter months. I can't help imagining I am reenacting the scene from *A Christmas Story*.

"I can't move my arms!"

"Move them when you get home."

The strain exacerbates my lower back pain: more ibuprofen, prescription pain medications, and muscle relaxants. Like my mother who had dealt with major back problems for decades, I accept the situation as part of life.

# CHAPTER 4

# WHY ME?

*(Debbie)*

While I was still in elementary school, the insidious root cause of my back pain first appeared in the guise of mysterious "kidney infections." As a high school freshman, birth control pills were prescribed to normalize irregular and painful menstrual cycles. Married at age twenty-one, a year later we decided to have a baby. After months of trying, my gynecologist asked a lot of questions, ordered various tests, and informed me it was highly unlikely I would ever conceive.

At age twenty-three, I was surprised to be pregnant. Three years later, in 1983, I was pregnant again, but the ache manifested itself in my lower left flank. Living in Virginia Beach at the time, Chuck's destroyer, *USS Arthur W. Radford* (DD-968), was in the Mediterranean. Actively involved in the fighting around Beirut, his ship was amongst the first to "fire in anger" since Vietnam.

At the Navy medical clinic in Norfolk, I expressed fears that my symptoms were not normal—that there was something seriously wrong with me. The doctor waved off my pain and concerns like I was an airplane attempting to land on the deck of a clobbered aircraft carrier (Clobbered means the flight deck is blocked by another airplane or whatever. I've learned a lot of great Navy lingo over the years.)

"You're a Navy wife under tremendous stress. Your husband is deployed to the other side of the world, and you're quite pregnant. You probably haul your son around on your hip. It's no mystery why your back is bothering you."

His explanation was plausible, but did not ring true. My gut knew better.

The young doctor wrote a quick prescription for Xanax, and moved on to his next patient. Xanax made me sleepy, dizzy, and spacey—a bad trio for the mother of a busy three-year-old. I soon quit the medication.

At that point, I had an epiphany: it was time to develop a backbone and take charge of my medical care. My rebellion against the traditional doctor-patient relationship—and implementation of my personal philosophy—began. Having always blindly trusted everything a doctor told me, I would no longer simply follow their proclamations. Every aspect of my medical care would be thoroughly researched and questioned by me until I understood what was going on. Trust, but verify. Physicians on my medical team would know me as a person, not simply as a set of symptoms encountering their lab coat. Medical professionals who would not interact with me on this level would not be included on my team. The inner place of knowledge, my gut instinct, had to be satisfied with the approach being taken to my medical care. It's amazing how often failure to listen to my inner voice screaming to do or not do something proved to be a mistake.

The nightly news regularly featured video of Chuck's ship firing into the Lebanese hillsides from a few thousand yards offshore. Subsequent news segments always included the wife or mother of some young sailor (usually stationed on the aircraft carrier), complaining about the perils faced by their service member. Such stories amused and disgusted my fellow Radford wives and me. I'm sure it wasn't very sensitive of us, but we loved mocking the pathetic looks and whimpers of the wives willing to appear on the local news.

"I don't know what I'm going to do if anything happens to him."

"What a bunch of crap! He's on the friggin' aircraft carrier—fifty miles away from the gunline! These women just want to get on the news," my friend Donna Murphy would say. "I saw her picking up sailors at the Chiefs' Club the same day her husband's ship pulled out!"

We were not sensitive to whining. It was great fun.

Informing Chuck of the news stories by mail required a few weeks to receive his reply:

*I've seen the most amazing sights here in Beirut. The first time I saw the city, as we approached from sea, it appeared modern and beautiful from a distance. But as we got closer, suddenly, we crossed a point from where the damage to the tall buildings, especially the Holiday Inn, became obvious. I realized from the stunned looks on the faces around me just how unaware we Americans are of the realities of war. Please, never embarrass me by complaining in a news interview...I volunteered to be where I am, and doing what I'm doing.*

After six months away, Chuck returned home just in time to witness Greg's birth in November of 1983. Since he missed the required training, my friend Donna Murphy acted as birthing coach. The next day—with my desired quota of children—I had my tubes tied. I was done birthing babies.

In 1985, I met with an endocrinologist at Strong Memorial Hospital in Rochester. My menstrual cycle had not occurred for nearly a year. He was moderately curious, and ordered several tests to check hormone levels and pituitary function. (He was not curious enough, however, to also check my adrenal function.) At twenty-nine I was improbably young to be post-menopausal, but I told myself that he was a specialist and his diagnosis of ovarian failure should carry some weight. *Wrong!* my gut screamed.

He prescribed estrogen replacement therapy to kick-start my menstrual cycle. Knowing inside this was a misdiagnosis—but not having a better solution—I took the hormones for several months until fear of potential cancer side effects justified quitting them. More children are not in my future, I reasoned, so what was the point in a menstrual cycle?

In fact, the thought of never having another period sounded good to me. Surprisingly, my menstrual cycle continued sporadically, disproving the ovarian failure diagnosis.

At the end of spring of 1989, Chuck received orders to *USS Lewis B. Puller* (FFG23)— its home port is Long Beach, California. We are viewing our pending move from Newport, Rhode Island to California as a new beginning for us. It has been nearly two years since my breast cancer diagnosis. Chuck will report to his new ship in November and serve as Engineering Officer. In the meantime, he completed Department Head School in July, and over the next few months will attend various engineering courses at Navy bases around the country.

My sister, Nancy, has invited us to stay with her in Corning, New York while Chuck hops around the country. She is getting married at the end of September, and I am going to be her Matron of Honor. It is exciting to be back in our hometown helping with wedding plans near friends and family.

While delivering Brian to a weeklong summer camp in the Adirondack Mountains, I am walking across an open field when I accidentally step into a rut. The act sends me to my knees on hard ground, twisting my ankle and jarring my back. So, in addition to a throbbing ankle, the chronic ache in my back cranks up to full volume. My mother-in-law, a nurse, witnesses the fall. The severity of the pain in my side does not seem normal to her. She encourages me to see a doctor. The pain level will subside to normal within a few days, I reason. The thought of wasting several hours in a doctor's waiting room to be prescribed ibuprofen causes me to resist.

Back at Nancy's house, I take plenty of self-prescribed ibuprofen. My ankle recovers, but the back pain grows worse. Every breath brings pain. Nancy takes over the job of pestering me to see a doctor.

"Maybe you need antibiotics for a bladder or kidney infection," she argues.

I relent and make the call. My urologist, from years ago, is out of town. His office refers me to a general practitioner filling in for him.

Arriving for my appointment, I am shocked by the size of the crowd in the waiting room. At Navy clinics, we refer to such mob scenes as a cattle call. The occasional *moo* always causes snickers. The room is over-flowing with patients, as many standing as seated. Tempted to moo, I abstain, figuring the humor won't play here in dairy country. Lucky to find an open section of wall, I brace my back against it. Controlling my breathing, I fight the urge to leave. After what seems an eternity, a seat opens. A quick look to make sure there are no standing old ladies as I dive for it.

When my name is called, I am disappointed to be examined by a physician's assistant. Voicing my desire to see the doctor, the P.A. apologizes.

"You're welcome to wait for the doctor, but I'm afraid it will be a long time before you get to see her. She is filling in for two doctors who are on vacation, and we are slammed. Seems the whole town is sick."

The thought of more hours in the waiting room causes me to acquiesce. Describing the back pain, I share my suspicions of the cause. She agrees my diagnosis is probably correct, and orders a urine test. Soon, I am informed my urine sample contains "cells consistent with a urinary tract infection."

With a prescription for antibiotics in hand, I leave the office. Once outside, my inner voice stops me in my tracks. Standing in the parking lot, watching as an approaching storm covers a patchy blue sky, I somehow know the diagnosis is wrong. Crazy, right? If my next move is to leave, I will be walking off a cliff. Listening to my gut, I rebel, and overcome the compliant part of me that is heading toward the pharmacy. A surge of strength turns me around and propels me back inside.

"Ma'am, I'm sorry, but I must insist on seeing the doctor," I say to the receptionist.

The doctor's gatekeeper examines me over her reading glasses and recognizes the immovability of my mindset.

Through a frown, she says, "Have a seat, Mrs. Wilson. I'm afraid it will be a while."

She clearly believes I am wasting everyone's time. Ignoring the part of me that hates to be a problem for anyone, I commit to the path demanded by my gut. Somehow, I know my life depends on it. I want to live so much, I am willing to be a pain in the butt.

At the end of the day, I have the waiting room to myself. I feel an odd sense of accomplishment as I survey my territory of empty seats and old magazines. At last, a nurse ushers me to an examining room. Climbing onto the end of a lightly padded examination table, the crunchy white paper puts me in mind of a butt-roast about to be wrapped up at a butcher shop. Noticing the holes into which stirrups for gynecological exams are inserted, I recall the humiliation of those exams. The paper crinkles as I shift my butt to alleviate the pain in my back. Where's the masking tape to seal me in? And black sharpie to write what sort of meat is in this package?

Dr. Pulcrabek enters the room. My reward for not having left: she is the most caring and compassionate doctor I have ever met. Despite a long day, her undivided attention is focused on me—time does not matter. Trying not to sound whiney, I tell her my husband is a naval officer, and that we are in the middle of a move to Southern California.

"I'm jealous!" she beams. "I sure wouldn't mind missing the winters we get around here."

Upon hearing of my breast cancer, she hugs me. Long suppressed concerns pour out. She listens as I recap my history of diagnoses and treatments.

"Mrs. Wilson, your test results do indicate a urinary tract infection, as my P.A. diagnosed. However, because of your medical history, I want to eliminate all other possibilities. We'll start with an abdominal ultrasound. If nothing else, we'll provide you with some peace of mind. Let's get it done right away at Corning Hospital. How does that sound?"

"Corning Hospital—that's where I was born!"

"Great!" she exclaims. "This will be something of a homecoming then."

"I'll try not to be a baby this time," I quip.

We laugh together, like friends.

Being from a small town has its perks. Most everyone is a friend or relative, or an acquaintance of a friend or relative. Such relationships provide opportunity for personalized attention. At Corning Hospital, a third cousin, Claudia Austin Putnam, whom I have not seen in many years, administers my ultrasound. Maneuvering a gel-covered wand back and forth over my abdomen, she pauses to click away on her computer keyboard as we laugh and reminisce.

Throughout the exam, I question what she is seeing. She points out certain organs on the screen, but informs me she cannot discuss any medical observations—good or bad. Her job is to complete the ultrasound examination and provide the results to the radiologist. He will study the report, share his findings with Dr. Pulcrabek, and she will share the information with me. Even though it all sounds perfectly proper, I want to know everything immediately.

The ultrasound does not provide enough information to satisfy Dr. Pulcrabek. She arranges for a special x-ray called an IVP that involves an intravenous injection. Learning more and more medical terminology, I'll soon be able to keep up with the best of them at cocktail parties. Dr. Pulcrabek says the IVP will give her a better image of my kidneys. Perhaps this procedure will help us determine the cause of what she describes as "referred pain." Excited and scared, I know we are on the verge of discovery.

During the IVP, Claudia pops her head into the x-ray room to inform the technician as to who I am.

"This is my cousin, Debbie Wilson. She used to be Debbie Pruden. She's related to the Austins, Prudens, and pretty much everyone else in the town of Campbell."

The technician grins and says, "My husband is great friends with your brother, Bobby...they've played softball together for years."

My mind is at ease, joking and laughing as the procedure is performed. Afterward, I happen into Claudia in the hallway. Her greeting is uncomfortable and sober.

"Do you know anything about the results of my scan?"

"Remember, I cannot discuss medical findings, good or bad. Results have to come from your doctor."

If there is one thing I am good at, it's questioning, and studying people to determine the truth of a matter. Maybe it's a skill that comes with being a mother. Already suspicious, I sense something in Claudia's evasiveness beyond her professional bearing. Insight dawns that something bad is being kept from me. Recognizing my obvious grasp of the truth and the resulting panic, Claudia volunteers to speak with the radiologist—maybe he will share his findings directly with me. She leaves me to check with him.

The radiologist steps into the hall, uncomfortable and displeased to be put in the spotlight. Radiologists normally function behind the scenes in dark little rooms, having little interaction with the people whose innermost aspects are their realm. Certain types of people tend toward functions in the medical backstage to avoid patient contact. They must figure it out during medical school.

Maybe it's the anxiety emanating from my face that softens him. Against the norm, he agrees to show me my x-rays. He escorts me to the dim room where he does his work. Large films with my name in the corner are plastered across a wide, backlit panel.

"Umm...your left kidney...appears to be...displaced downward."

He points to the shades of gray denoting my left kidney. Even I can perceive it is in a lower position than the right kidney.

"What would cause something like this?" I press.

Using an index finger to circle objects among the film's shadows: "The guilty party...this grapefruit-sized mass...above the kidney."

I gasp.

He closes up tight like a clam sensing danger, and refuses to discuss my x-ray further. At age thirty-three, the perpetrator that my body has been harboring since childhood is brought into the light.

"I will send my report to your doctor. She will explain the findings. I should not be having this conversation with you."

Scared beyond belief, I am also vindicated. Years spent questioning and attempting to alert physicians, in major medical facilities around the country, about my back pain scroll before me. Savoring the rich irony that Dr. Pulcrabek—a small-town general practitioner who accepts what my medical insurance remits as full payment—is the one to finally figure out my condition. Everything has become clear to me. She has saved my life because she listened to me and took the initiative to investigate. Part of me revels in the fact I have been right all along, not carcinoma-phobic. There is something quite large—the size of a grapefruit—in my abdomen.

"What's so friggin' hard about finding something the size of a damn grapefruit when I've pointed to the exact spot for so many doctors?" I almost scream to my mother and sister at dinner.

The next day, Dr. Pulcrabek describes the mass as being in the area of my left adrenal gland, and the size of a large softball. At least she isn't ruining fruit for me. Adrenal glands, she informs me, are normally the size of a walnut. Oh well, there goes one of the nut family. Without further tests, she cannot confirm whether the mass is a benign growth or some type of cancer.

Not wanting to disturb his studies, I keep Chuck completely in the dark as to what I am going through. He is attending an engineering school at Great Lakes Naval Training Center, north of Chicago.

He arrives at my sister's house beaming with homecoming happiness. His expression turns to shocked disbelief with my bad news, and then an obvious state of agony. As expected, he is upset with me for keeping him in the dark. However, I understand the workings of his mind. My medical situation provides a special exemption from any consequences. He forgives me in an instant.

The next step is to travel two hours to Rochester for a CT scan with intravenous contrast. My mass is given the name "adrenal tumor." My urine is collected for a twenty-four hour period and sent to California for testing.

"My pee is going to make it to California before I do," I joke—desperate for a laugh.

It is essential to know whether my adrenal tumor is functioning or non-functioning. A functioning tumor can release a rush of hormones during removal, causing the heart to race out of control. Death would come quickly on the operating table. Thoughts of that possibility race through my brain, keeping me awake at night. To my great relief, the tumor is found to be non-functioning. The remaining question is whether the mass is cancerous or benign.

It is now the end of August, and word has come that I will undergo surgery on September 8th. Assisting Nancy with her wedding plans distracts me. There will be three weeks for me to recover before walking down the aisle as Matron of Honor. Holding tight to that vision and making it a reality becomes my primary goal. Nancy is one of my greatest cheerleaders. She is working extra hard to keep my spirits up during these days of waiting. Between her sense of humor—and the prescribed narcotics—the pain and tension are tolerable.

My dress arrives at the bridal shop, but I delay having it fitted. My weight and shape are about to change.

My husband is my source for solutions and hope—guy stuff. Together, we figure out big challenges are best faced with a tough personal philosophy. The bigger the adversary, the stronger and sharper our inner weapons must be. Chuck fans the flames of my defiant anger.

Cancer is not going to plow me under! Steeling myself to have the "thing" removed, and recover quickly, I will participate in my sister's wedding and move on with life on my terms. Rallying around Nancy's wedding and our pending move to California, I will not accept the common-sense reality of death by cancer. Listening only to hopeful thoughts of survival, I will get through the month with the fewest ripples; the fewest concessions possible to cancer.

My philosophy: Find footing where most refuse to fight; deny cancer its rumored omnipotence.

Chuck and I arrive back at Genesee Hospital early on the 7th of September 1989, which is also Nancy's birthday. Dr. Penn will, once again, perform as my surgeon.

Placed in a semi-private room, my roommate is a young woman also here to have an abdominal tumor removed. Her surgery is scheduled for later this morning. Chuck sits beside my bed, holding my hand while I chat with my neighbor.

"Are you a Christian?" she asks.

The question takes me by surprise.

"Umm, yes," I reply, uncomfortable.

Considering myself a Christian, I never want to be too creepy about it—that is, bring it up in conversation. Especially with people I know. Or strangers. Does that include everyone?

Before the orderlies arrive to take her to surgery, I listen through the curtain as my roommate's parents pray with her.

"Good luck," I offer as she is wheeled out, followed by her mother and father. She beams a peaceful smile back at me.

"Christians can be so odd," I say to Chuck.

We are relieved to have the room to ourselves.

It is late afternoon when my roommate is returned to the room. She is in obvious discomfort, and I hear soft moans during her transfer from the gurney to her bed. Her parents arrive as she settles in. They nod and smile infinite peace as they pass through my *heathen* side of the room.

"It must run in the family," I wisecrack.

Her folks are hair-trigger attentive throughout the afternoon and evening whenever their daughter utters a sound. Doctors come and go. Nurses make their rounds. The darkness outside, covered by our reflections, fills the large windows. When it is announced visiting hours are over, Mom and dad stand next to their daughter, say quiet prayers, and gather their belongings. Stopping briefly at the foot of my bed, they promise to pray for me, and smile from their safe places in forever as they walk out the door.

"I want whatever it is they're on," I joke in a close whisper to Chuck.

"They're high on Jesus," Chuck replies, a bit too loud.

"*Shh*," I warn.

Chuck lingers until a nurse personally informs him visiting hours are over. The rest of the night is quiet except for the moans of my roommate whenever she shifts position. Scared and alone, I pray for myself.

The shock of bright lights snapped on by hospital staff awakens me. It's my turn—my trip to the operating room. From across my roommate's bed, the window once again reflects the room from the blackness beyond. Chuck is next to me.

"Honey, everything is going to be fine," he promises. "See you after the operation."

We hold each other for a moment. Surprise...the hallway outside my room is filled with my family. Tears pour from my eyes at the sight. They arose at an awful hour this morning to make the two-hour drive in time to see me off to surgery. Crying, I thank them. It feels so good to have them here for me, and to stand vigil with Chuck. Laughing and joking, they escort my gurney to the elevator where they blow kisses and say their see-you-laters. In the holding room, an I.V. is started. The drug administered calms my anxiety, and I doze off quickly.

Gasping for air, I awaken in a room without windows. A mask is placed over my mouth.

"Breath," I am told.

Drifting in and out of consciousness, recovery room attendants keep watch over me. Spasms of pain rip through my abdomen with each conscious breath. Back at my room, I am hoisted onto my bed with a myriad of tubes and monitors attached. It is dark outside. I have missed the entire day.

A few family members are in my room, tired and somber. Questioning them, I learn the surgery went long. My left adrenal gland and kidney were removed, along with a large grapefruit-sized tumor. We are back on the fruit thing.

My abdomen continues to spasm. There is no relief from the tidal waves of torment.

Communicating is difficult. My family decides to leave, saying I will be less agitated and rest better without their presence. Chuck feels especially terrible. He is scheduled to fly to San Francisco in the morning to attend a weeklong shipboard firefighting school on Treasure Island Naval Base. He was not prepared to see me in so much pain, and is having serious second thoughts about leaving. We argue.

Stubborn, I insist, "Go...go...you have to go."

He relents.

It is a horrible night as I thrash and moan. Wishing Chuck hadn't left, that he had refused me and stayed, I cry, making things worse. The more I tense, the worse the pain; the worse the pain, the more I tense. My abdomen feels as if it is being twisted and wrung out like a dishcloth. The cycle of torture is relentless. Coming out of delirium, I become aware of the noise I am creating, making it difficult for my roommate to get any rest.

She is awake because I hear her speaking to someone. Who could be visiting her at this hour of the night?

She isn't talking to another person. She is praying.

She is praying for me.

Listening to her words, I let go, allowing myself to float on her prayers. I picture myself in the arms of Jesus. I sleep. Waking in the light, a feeling of peace is passing through me like the morning sunshine streaming through our window onto my roommate and me. The muscle spasms have eased; reminded of them only when I move.

Later in the day, I am taken to radiology for a CT of the chest. A routine x-ray, done before my surgery, revealed a spot on my right lung. Experiencing off-the-scale pain as I am transferred to a gurney, then onto the narrow slab of the CT machine. There is talk of performing a needle biopsy—the thought nearly sends me over the edge. Even the idea of one more procedure is intolerable. Back in my room, I await word from the doctors.

Chuck's weeklong absence during my recovery is hard on both of us. Speaking on the phone each evening, we remind each other of our plans. The future we have worked so hard to organize will make the separation worthwhile. Besides, it is part of our rebellion against cancer. Our philosophy is ringing a bit hollow with him away at such a time, but I am surrounded by supportive family. Everything is going to be fine; our boys are well cared for by my sister and mother, I tell myself.

Chuck's absence is not popular with some well-meaning members of my family. They don't understand our sacrifice. They see the difficulty of my recovery, and believe Chuck to be hard-hearted for being far away at such a time. We considered asking the Navy to adjust his timetable, but feared the disruption would cause the loss of his duty assignment and necessitate a new set of orders. If asked, the Navy would certainly be sympathetic of our situation, making whatever changes deemed necessary. However, even a well-meaning bureaucratic hand should be avoided.

We have invested a good deal of time, effort, and emotional energy into our pending move to the L.A./Long Beach area. Navy housing has been arranged, and the school our children will attend investigated. Rossmoor Elementary in Los Alamitos has an excellent reputation. We might not be so fortunate, school-wise, if Chuck's orders were changed to a different ship and home port location. Besides, we have already grown tired of cancer's way of taking the wheel, and steering its course into our future. We decided to take a stand as part of our insurgency against the cancer regime.

Word comes regarding the suspicious area on my lung. They located a chest x-ray taken prior to my breast cancer surgery two years ago. The spot was there then, and hasn't changed. The radiologist determines the spot to be a nipple shadow, and decides against doing a biopsy. Relieved by the explanation, the shadow passes from my thoughts.

At the end of the week, Chuck returns from San Francisco. Having him near renews my strength. He does not know what to make of my story of the night my roommate prayed for me.

The urologist called upon during my surgery to remove my left kidney stops by my room. Seeing I am awake, he enters and asks how I am feeling. Seating himself in a chair beyond the foot of my bed, he makes small talk while searching for the words to explain the pathology results.

"The tumor was cancerous, a very rare type called adrenal cortical carcinoma. In all my years of practice, this is the first such case I have ever seen. There is no effective chemotherapy. Radiation is not an option. Surgical removal of the tumor is the standard method of treatment. There was nothing more to be done.

"The tumor was the size of a large grapefruit, totally encapsulated by a thick rind-like cover. That is a good thing, as it allowed me to remove the tumor intact. I regret that I had to remove your otherwise healthy kidney, but the tumor was simply too firmly attached.

"That tumor must have been around for several years as it contained bone-like areas of calcification. That indicates it probably grew at times, and then went dormant for periods. Somehow, your body's defense mechanisms kept it in check."

While I hate to hear I have another cancer, at least there is an explanation for the many health issues I have experienced in my life.

"I also had to remove your spleen. Pressure from the tumor had turned it to mush."

"What does all of this mean?" I ask him. "Am I going to be okay? What is the next step? What is the life span of a person diagnosed with adrenal cancer?"

His reply stuns me.

"I don't know...you could live for a couple months or you could live for up to five or even ten years...it all depends on whether I was able to get all of the cancer."

He pauses for a moment, and positions himself squarely in his chair. Obviously, he is about to deliver some difficult news.

"Now..." he begins, "I need to be perfectly frank with you. If this cancer has spread to any other organ in your body, the survival rate for adrenal cortical carcinoma is particularly poor beyond five years. Based on the large size of your primary tumor, it has almost certainly spread. As to what this all means—you will most likely see metastatic tumors appear in your lungs, liver, or bones at some point. If there is anything to be thankful for, your body seems to have somehow kept the growth of this cancer in check. So far, you have had remarkably few side effects. With so much uncertainty, I highly recommend you get your affairs in order."

My only response as I digest what I heard is to stare at him. He takes my silence as his cue to leave—job done.

"Sorry to be the bearer of such bad news."

Alone, with few words being spoken, Chuck and I begin to comprehend the enormity of what we have been told. Panic engulfs me. I do the only thing left to do...I pray. Pleading with God to make it all go away, I bargain—offer—to do anything if he will just let me live to raise my children. How many times in the past have I promised to be more faithful to him, to be a better, kinder person, to go to church regularly, to quit drinking alcohol?

Despite the things I learned about my relationship with God after my breast cancer, I reverted to my old way of thinking. What a laugh. My faith is so immature, so superstitious. Since childhood, I have been afraid doing something wrong will incur God's wrath. I believed if I did and said the right things, dressed the right way, went to church, then I would be good with God. Only my actions mattered. Thus, I am angry with myself. Obviously, I am a disappointment to God and being punished for something I have or have not done. I deserve what is happening to me. From this perspective, I continue to pray, promising God I will change, bargaining future actions on my part for current actions on his part.

Promising to do anything to be around to see my children grow up, I am driven by a question: who *could* or would ever love them as much as me, their mother? God knows, I am correct on that point. The thought of not being part of their lives brings overwhelming sadness, and I weep as the words of the doctor replay in my mind. Having beaten breast cancer, now I am facing a completely different variety. Isn't one cancer per customer enough? Praying, I cry foul until exhaustion delivers sleep.

During my ten days in the hospital, I set small goals each day. Day one, with help getting out of bed, I shuffle to the door. Day two, I gingerly make my way to the nurses' station. Bent over like a little old lady, I push my I.V. pole, and tote a paper bag hiding my catheter and urine bag, venturing out a little further each time. Exploring the floor, I discover a connecting hallway with a cushioned bench that faces a wall of windows. I make my way there often, pausing to rest or cry and, sometimes, pray. I ache to go home. Thoughts of Nancy's upcoming wedding goad me to keep walking.

Upon discharge from the hospital, I can't yet stand up straight, but on the plus side I have lost twenty pounds. My mother spends the days with me at Nancy's house, encouraging me in her gentle way to get out and walk a little further each day. Perseverance pays off. Three weeks after surgery, minus my left kidney and various other body parts, I walk down the aisle as Nancy's Matron of Honor and dance at the reception. Having lost so much weight, I look great.

# CHAPTER 5

# CALIFORNIA, HERE WE COME

*(Debbie)*

The day after Nancy's wedding, Chuck and my brother Bob load our two vehicles and depart for California with Brian and Greg. Unable to travel by car, my mother and I will fly to LAX. The day before I arrive, our household goods are delivered to our assigned military housing unit. Chuck, by himself, puts the beds together, sets furniture in general locations, and unpacks as many kitchen boxes as possible before picking us up at the airport. Walking into a house of randomly deposited furniture, surrounded by stacks of unopened boxes, I am overwhelmed. Not physically able to settle an entire household, I am especially anxious as Chuck is due to leave for Korea within a week to meet his ship.

Working long and hard during his remaining days with me, Chuck gets the place whipped into shape. While my mother cannot help much physically, her encouragement and sense of humor assist our rapid progress. It is October 1989, and Mom will stay with us through March 1990. Wherever we are living, Chuck always encourages Mom to stay for as long as she wants. Memories of her extended visits are precious to me.

Living in Los Alamitos, we are within a few miles of Long Beach Naval Hospital. There, I am assigned to Commander Robert Leyse, M.D., a sixty-two year old thoracic surgeon recently retired from his civilian practice. He seems out of place with his white hair and obvious maturity among Navy doctors who tend to be quite young.

He responds with a humorous spark to my clumsy question as to why he joined the Navy at his age.

"Because it's not just a job, it's an adventure," he says, quoting the Navy recruiting slogan.

From our initial meeting, I am impressed with Dr. Leyse. It is my first experience with a doctor who has taken the time to get ready for an appointment with a patient. In fact, based on his questions and comments, I can tell he has studied my already massive medical record in detail. Having grown used to the lazy, "So, how can I help you today?" approach typical of so many doctors, I am stunned by his professionalism. Beyond being prepared, he exudes experience which, combined with his personal warmth and interest in my case, make me feel special.

From that first encounter, he adds dimensions and depth to my situational understanding.

"It's fairly rare for someone your age to have had two primary cancers. In all my years in medicine, you are the first person I have ever met with adrenal cortical carcinoma."

He assesses me for a moment before piling up the statistics.

"As rare as it is, I suspect many oncologists work their way through an entire career without a case. I'm going to do someone a favor, and refer you to a local civilian oncologist. I will need their help to stay on top of your case."

Turns out, Dr. Leyse is right; the Long Beach oncologist I meet with is in his fifties, and I am his first adrenal cancer patient. As odd as it sounds, I find myself feeling quite exceptional because of the rarity of my disease. Surreal.

"The CT scan they took this morning was clear of any problems in the area of your recent surgery. However, I am concerned about something on your chest x-ray."

Dr. Leyse indicates an x-ray film displayed against a panel lit up on the wall. I am surprised by what I see.

"What are all those bright spots?" I ask, pointing at a cluster of white rectangles.

"Oh, those are the surgical clips holding things together where you used to have a kidney, spleen, gallbladder, and adrenal gland."

"Gallbladder? They took out my gallbladder?"

"Yes. Didn't they tell you?"

"Maybe. It's all a bit of a blur."

Still coming to terms with the amount of metal in my abdomen, and the fact that I didn't know I no longer have a gallbladder, he shifts my focus.

"There is a shadow here on your right lung," he says, tapping the offender with the top of his pen.

After a lightning bolt of fright, I recall what the radiologist said a few months earlier in Rochester.

"Oh, that spot is a nipple shadow," I report with the confidence of a medical professional.

"Nipple shadow, hmm? If that were the case, Dr. Debra, wouldn't it have a twin?" he quizzes with a raised eyebrow.

With a gotcha grin under a crown of gray hair, he taps the film like a snare drum. Obvious, even to my untrained eye, the proportionally appropriate region on the other side of my chest x-ray is void of a matching shadow.

Beyond my depth, the heat of embarrassment evaporates my *medical credentials*. In full blush, a part of me cannot give up—the part that must always have the last word. I flail to keep my head above water.

"Well," I stammer, "a few months ago, the radiologist in Rochester saw that same spot, and...well, he was concerned too...but then he found that same spot on a two-year-old x-ray, and it...it hadn't changed. He said it was a...a nipple shadow."

The more I speak, the more I know from the amused look on Dr. Leyse's face I am relating something stupid, but I can't stop. One of the things I fear most is being wrong.

Clearly enjoying—but also sensitive to—my embarrassment, Dr. Leyse says, "I'm sorry, Debbie. I know you didn't come up with the nipple shadow thing on your own. Conclusions that ridiculous require several years of medical school."

His consoling smile reveals the warmth in his heart. Letting down my defenses, I allow myself to accept and trust him.

"Okay, Debbie, I want to help you get things into proper perspective. I'm sure your mind is jumping to the conclusion this is another cancer, but, there are plenty of other explanations for that nodule. Noncancerous possibilities. In fact, it is unlikely to be another cancer. If it were not for your medical history, I might allow myself to dismiss that shadow with an explanation as goofy as the one our doctor friend in Rochester came up with.

"Now, as the Good Lord said, 'Worry never added a day to anyone's life.' So, be encouraged. Whatever it is, it has been there in your lung for at least two years with little or no change. At least your radiologist in Rochester got that part right. However, I am going to request those old x-rays for comparison purposes. We need to keep a close watch on your nipple shadow."

Blushing again, we laugh together.

Southern California has everything. We live within eight miles of Disneyland, and a few miles from the beach. The weather is always fantastic. Sometimes, snow covered mountains are visible through what we call the "Jell-O 1-2-3" layers of smog. The L.A./Long Beach area is sensory overload for a girl from rural upstate New York. I push the lung issue out of my mind and take advantage of the opportunities available in Southern California.

While Brian and Greg are in school during the day, I scout out the locale with my mother. Physical fitness could enhance my chances of survival, so we have joined a nearby fitness club and work out there every day, religiously. Mom loves the pool and spa. Participating in aerobics classes and using the exercise equipment are my thing. Sporting my wedding day weight, I am the happiest I have been with my appearance in many years.

When Chuck's ship returns to Long Beach from deployment, I plan to leave our boys with my mother and take him to a hotel. Mom is appalled I would do such a thing. After all, he has not seen the boys in months.

"They will survive one more day without seeing their dad. I want him all to myself for one night. Besides, I am finally feeling good—much better than when he left."

Even after his homecoming, Chuck's job as Chief Engineer is going to keep him away from home a good deal of the time. Thankfully, several Navy wives in the neighborhood have become very good friends and my support system.

It's March of 1990, my mother is returning home to New York, and I'm returning to the naval hospital. The follow-up chest x-ray shows the spot on my lung has grown.

Standing next to Dr. Leyse, he compares my most recent x-ray to the one taken six months prior. Side-by-side on a lit-up panel, the films reveal that long ago my life took an unwanted turn. Using a small metal ruler, he demonstrates how much my so-called nipple shadow has increased in size. Not a lot, but measurable.

"Let's not jump to worst case conclusions. This can still be some sort of benign activity, and even if it's cancer, it's almost certainly adrenal—in your case, slow growing. It's as if you and adrenal cancer have a 'you don't bother me; I won't bother you' agreement. Breast cancer is much more aggressive. We would not be having this conversation if it were breast cancer."

"Small comfort—slow, but sure," I reason.

In my heart, I know it is cancer. Stage 4 adrenal cancer. The weight of a heavy shadow falls over me.

Perceptive of my state of mind, Dr. Leyse leads me to his office, sits me down, and calmly describes my options.

"You can choose to wait, do nothing, and keep an eye on the lesion with regular chest x-rays. We could try to get a biopsy. That will be a bit tricky, and we might not get the right tissue. Or I can remove the nodule surgically. Even if it is a benign growth, it will probably need to be removed at some point."

He further explains the risks of each choice, and gives me time to absorb the information.

"What do you think I should do?" I ask.

"I'm a surgeon, my dear. My motto is, 'if in doubt, take it out.'"

"What if I were your daughter?"

"I just gave you the advice I would give you if you were my daughter," he says, and I know he means it.

"Go home. Discuss your options with your family. Whatever it is, it has been there for a long while. There is no rush. Take a little time to make your decision. I'm sorry this is happening."

Before I leave his office, Dr. Robert Leyse hugs me like I really am his daughter.

The importance of establishing a personal relationship with my doctors is so clear to me now. Because of our growing friendship, Dr. Leyse develops a genuine interest in me as a human being. He wants to know what is going on in my life. He makes himself available when I need him, provides carefully thought-out answers, and even draws pictures in response to my many queries. He is patient with me in his no-nonsense way. Following his advice, I decide to have the lung lesion surgically removed.

The post-surgery pathology report proves adrenal cancer metastasized to another organ many years ago. My already thin sense of security is shattered. A wrecking ball, swung by someone peering at my cells through the lens of a microscope, destroys the facade that was my *healthy* life.

It's official, I have been bumped into an all-capital-letter category: STAGE 4 CANCER.

The odds of surviving stage 4 cancer are slim. Where else have tumor cells migrated? My liver? My bones?

Desperate to believe the lung nodule to be the only metastatic cancer in my body, I take the Scarlett O'Hara approach of, "I'll think about it tomorrow," but stage 4 cancer has taken up unwelcome residence in my mind where it sprawls out on the furniture, leaves empty pizza boxes, cigarette butts, and beverage bottles strewn among my thoughts.

There is no follow-up radiation or chemotherapy. Surgery remains the standard treatment for adrenal cancer. Scans every three to six months become a routine part of my life.

Needing hope, I decide it is time to get involved in a faith community. Broken and distressed beyond my ability to cope, I am even willing to go to church.

At the invitation of a neighbor, the boys and I visit a local United Methodist Church, and find it quite welcoming. Wearing down Chuck's resistance, he accompanies us when his ship is not at sea. Praying for God to change his heart, I lack faith that such a change will happen.

"All things are possible with God." Chuck's attitude shifts. It begins with his acknowledgement that the pastor delivers powerful, thought-provoking sermons. He enjoys the meet-and-greets after the service. Over coffee, he finds our fellow parishioners and the pastors to be much different than the holy rollers he expected.

Change continues when we become involved in an adult Sunday School class. The basis of the class is parenting. We meet wonderful, fun couples. We look forward to sharing stories of our latest parenting challenges, and always receive the advice and encouragement we need. Our social activities begin to center around church activities and our circle of church friends. Family retreat weekends at a rustic church camp in the San Bernardino Mountains are great fun. Our church family becomes our sustaining lifeblood as the Navy moves us around the country. God gathered us into his arms just in time to shelter us from storms to come.

# CHAPTER 6

# A MOVING TARGET

*(Debbie)*

Scrolling down the list of twenty-four hour periods in my life that have achieved "worst-day-ever" status causes my head to shake in disbelief. The field of competitors for this terrible distinction includes several formidable runners-up as well. My first breast cancer ranked supreme for two years before being soundly beaten by adrenal cancer. Next to spend time at the top of the list was the day I was diagnosed with stage-four adrenal cancer. Death stood close that day. The second breast cancer, this time in my right breast, was an annoying speed-bump, but my double-mastectomy had its day in the sun. Waking from surgery without breasts hit me hard and made it difficult to feel like a real woman.

"You're my Velveteen Rabbit," Chuck would say and then hold me tight.

Reconstructive surgery and Chuck's unwavering love and prayer helped my outlook.

Then, in August of 1993, a new low point of my life rose to the top, so to speak. Within days of our move to Eldridge, Iowa from Southern California, we were still buzzing with excitement about our first ever newly-built home. During our first meeting with my new oncologist at University of Iowa Medical Center, my day was destroyed. Based on a troubling CT scan performed that morning, the oncologist requested a consult with an oncology surgeon. That day is forever etched in my memory.

"There are over a dozen adrenal tumors spread throughout your liver, Mrs. Wilson. Your situation is inoperable. I wouldn't touch you with a ten-foot pole," says the surgeon as he pokes at several dark spots on the illuminated CT scan film displayed on the wall before us.

The words "over a dozen tumors," "inoperable," and "ten-foot pole" ping-pong around in my brain. Useless, I am glad when the surgeon and his arrogant manner leave the room. On his way to ruin someone else's day, I assume.

Then, the oncologist says the last words anyone ever wants to hear from a doctor.

"Mrs. Wilson, I must advise you to go home, and get your affairs in order."

This is my second time receiving "The Talk." Days when you receive "The Talk" always take their place at the top of the worst-day-ever list for a while. It's a rule.

"How long do I have?"

"There is no way to know for sure, but I would expect you might have six or as many as twelve months before the growth of the tumors cause serious symptoms and impact your quality of life. Once that occurs, things will progress quite quickly."

He allows time for his words to sink in.

"Most people given this news decide to use their period of relative health, before the tumors get too large, to travel, and spend time with family. You're still strong! Do the things you have always *wanted* to do while you still can."

Defiant, I say, "I've always *wanted* to grow old with my husband!"

Through tears, I lament, "I have two young sons who need me. I can't leave them without a mother. I've seen people go through the final stages of cancer—I know exactly what it is like. I can't stand the thought of a slow, painful death."

"Mrs. Wilson, we have greatly improved our approach to pain management," he offers. "For too many years, standard practice has been to use pain medications sparingly. We were worried about people becoming addicted. That's crazy when dealing with a terminal patient."

The word "terminal" caused a renewed burst of tears. It's such an awful word. Despite obvious experience, this oncologist is all-thumbs when handling bad news.

"That means I will be so drugged-up and out of it at the end of my life I won't know anybody!" I almost scream.

Angry, my mind is processing this information from a numb, insulated place. If I take it in, really expose myself to the reality of it, I will melt—fall apart. I can't do that.

"Let's go, honey. Let's go home," Chuck says, and helps me to my feet.

Visibly moved by our distress, the oncologist stops us as we are about to walk out of the examining room.

"I don't want to give you false hope, but I will present your case to the transplant board during their meeting this afternoon. We have a new organ transplant team here at the hospital headed up by a liver specialist. She will be at the meeting. Once again, I caution you, do not get your hopes up. You have stage-four cancer. That makes you a poor candidate for transplant.

"Mrs. Wilson, you have already lived longer than just about anyone ever with adrenal cancer because your body has a strong auto-immune system. Like I've said before, you are healthy, except for the cancer.

"The problem is," he continues, "to prevent the rejection of a transplanted organ, your auto-immune system would have to be suppressed. Doing so would allow any stray cancer cells in your body to run unchecked. The transplant committee will not want to risk wasting an organ on someone with stage-four cancer if there is a better candidate. Believe me, there is always a long list of people waiting for transplant."

We accept his point and leave the hospital without hope.

As Chuck drives, looking out at the world, I say, "How can this be? Look at all these cars...people going about their lives as if nothing is wrong. I've just been told I'm going to die soon."

Shell-shocked, we say very little on the ride home. Tears roll down my face as I mull my second death sentence over and over in my mind. Get my affairs in order. Enjoy my remaining six months of relative health before a steep decline greased with liberal use of morphine to control pain until I slide through death's door. My kids will grow up without a mother. Chuck will find someone else. This sucks!

Arriving home, I retreat to our freshly painted master bedroom, alone. Desperate and crying, I plead with God for more life; for a sign that he, the heralded creator of the universe, is on the receiving end of my prayers. A big part of me is angry with God over the fact I have cancer at all. What have I done to deserve this? Am I wasting my time praying? What if you do not exist? What if you are just so much fluff? Should I spend the final months of my life a silly devotee to a myth?

I am so angry that the truth of God's existence can only be known after death, and then only if he and an afterlife exist—a maddening conundrum. It bothers me that my prayers and desire for him to be real are partly motivated by base jealousy. My gut houses trepidation that, at some point following my death, I will be replaced in the minds of my sons by a stepmother. I hate myself for thinking this way—can't help it.

Desiring to prevent my demise, I beg for a miracle, a miracle tailored to suit my bitter outlook. "Lord, I'll do anything if you keep me alive long enough to witness both my children graduating high school. Please, they must *always* think of *me* as their mother!"

The math, however—as callously calculated by the 800-pound gorilla in the room—mocks the unbounded foolishness of my request. Let's see, Greg, my youngest son, is nine years old. I need nine years to see him wear a mortarboard on his head. The doctor said I have a year— at most. Even if God is real, and listening, my appeal is outrageous. My death will be rough on my family, but memory of me will fade, existing only in fleeting thoughts on special days in the future. My husband will have someone else on his arm remarking how proud she is of *my* sons. Resentment devolves into storms of raging hatred for an unnamed candidate filling my shoes, then myself for being so hateful.

For some reason, the notion occurs to open my Bible at a random page and drop my finger onto a verse. Like a drowning swimmer, I am grasping for anything within reach. So, ridiculous as it sounds, I reach for God, attempting to force him to seize my hand before slipping beneath the surface, forever. What I read knocks the scales from my eyes, struck with a revelation that changes everything, and turns my world upside down. If today marks the low point of my life, it also contains the highest.

My finger, wet with tears, sticks to the fine gilt-edged paper, exactly underlining these words in Psalm 128:6: "...and may you live to see your children's children."

I could not be more stunned if a monkey were to appear and randomly bang out those same words on the old Royal typewriter we still carry around the country. Perhaps God, as portrayed in Michelangelo's painting in the Sistine Chapel, has been straining to reach me my whole life. Have I simply failed to reach in his direction?

With the Bible pressed between my finger and palm, I barely touch the stairs on my descent.

"Chuck," I shout with a tingling of spiritual excitement I have never before experienced. "Look, read this. I'm going to be okay. Somehow, I know I'm going to be okay."

"What?" Chuck says, his face a question mark as he observes my manic behavior. Then, he focuses his field of vision just about my finger.

"Read it so you don't think I'm crazy."

"...and may you live to see your children's children."

He tries to hold me but I am too excited—jumping up and down. Chuck struggles to come to grips with what has just happened, a miracle.

The phone rings. I grab the phone, jubilant.

"Hello."

"Hello, Mrs. Wilson, this is Deb Tarara, Nurse Coordinator for Dr. Maureen Martin, head of the transplant team here at University of Iowa Medical Center. Dr. Martin would like to meet with you at your earliest convenience. She has a treatment idea she wants to discuss with you."

Hanging up the phone, I begin the most joyful scream of my life.

"God has revealed himself to us. He is real!" I shout and bounce around the house like Tigger from Winnie the Pooh.

I know it is possible to happen upon all sorts of verses in the Bible I would have found supportive at that moment, but for me, this event—this verse—is too powerful and specific to be explained away as feeble coincidence. A moment ago, I was ready to discard the whole Christianity mess. I wanted vengeance, for God to be dead; religion gone from my mind, and my life cleansed of ancient hocus pocus relics. Instead, from somewhere outside my understood reality, God broke into my heart. God has enigmatically chosen to respond to my nonsensical rant with an implausible promise. Right now, when I am in the running for the last person on earth to deserve him.

God has acknowledged my petition, and radically upped the ante. In my mind, with my medical history, the concept of meeting my grandchildren exists far too distant from my orbit to comprehend, to distinguish from any other star in this universe I am about to leave. In my rowdy congress of competing thoughts, rational judgements shout to gain the floor, to reign me in.

"Preposterous!"

"Impossible!"

"Your newfound faith is based on a crazy coincidence."

"You're being silly!"

"You have stage-four adrenal cortical carcinoma. Rare, and always deadly; there's no effective chemotherapy. The surgeon told you it's inoperable. Even radiation is not an option. Transplant—never! It's in your liver, for God's sake!"

"Get your affairs in order."

In the face of these sensible positions, a grassroots groundswell rises from the ashes and elects a new party to majority status. I choose to believe in God's promise and existence. His first act is the granting of grace, and a sense of peace far beyond logic. Breathing deep, the boot of oppressive thoughts lifts from my neck; hope fills my lungs.

Logic tries to build a wall, to make me reticent about sharing the story of my promise. The good news is—akin to the dinosaurs of Jurassic Park—my story, my experience is too potent for any fence.

"What the heck," I argue with my common sense, "if I'm wrong, if I'm crazy, if this really was a fluke occurrence, I will only have six to twelve months to be embarrassed. But, if it's true, as I know it is, I have a responsibility to report it; to share the good news."

How would I respond to hearing this reality story from someone else, I wonder? Would I listen uncomfortably and excuse their conspicuous wackiness? After all, the poor person has cancer. Or, would I accept what a lone survivor tells me as a revelation of God? I seriously doubt it.

## CHAPTER 7

# FROM FEAR TO FAITH

### *(Chuck)*

I t's 1997. In a little curtained-off space in the pre-op staging area, I am holding Debbie's hand. Her grip tightens, and body stiffens with the arrival of two members of the surgical team. Wearing green scrubs and skullcaps, cloth masks hanging from their necks, they verify Debbie's identity against the information on their clipboard.

"What's your date of birth, Mrs. Wilson?"

"Five, twenty-three, fifty-six," she responds.

"What is the purpose of your surgery today?"

"My surgeon is going to remove about thirty percent of my liver."

"That's correct! You've just won a trip to the O.R.," the one with the clipboard quips with a self-assured smile.

The men assume positions at the head and foot of her narrow gurney, and release the wheel brakes with a *click, click*. Our goodbye will serve as the signal for them to wheel her to the operating room.

Debbie, her fine brown hair hidden by a puffy-blue, hospital-issued hair cover, is trembling. My breathing becomes shallow. Leaning over the gurney's safety-rail, I kiss her.

"Everything is going to be fine," I promise. Looking up at the attendant nearest her head, I say, "She always gets panicky prior to surgery."

The individual near her feet replies, smiling, "We'll give her a little something to calm her down in a jiff. I will contact you in the waiting room with an update midway through the surgery—in about two hours."

"I will see you after," I say, connecting with the scared look in her brown eyes.

"I love you," she says, then shifts to an authoritative tone, "Don't forget to take my dad for a walk."

"Yes, my queen," I reply with a bow.

She curls her lower lip out, her way of saying, "Here goes, even though I would much rather not."

Even more beautiful than the day I married her, she is the picture of health. Except for the cancer, she is in excellent physical shape. Through diet, exercise, and supplements, she has enhanced her body's ability to fight the disease. Soon her abdomen will be open for inspection. I let go of her hand, and concentrate on my breathing as she disappears through a set of automatic doors labeled, "Authorized Personnel Only Beyond This Point."

This is a familiar scene for us. Debbie has endured twelve major surgeries, and numerous other biopsies and procedures at close intervals during the past nine years. The psychological impact of so many battles with cancer causes her body to react with shaking and nausea, even when just visiting a friend in the hospital.

"There's an odor that sets me off," she always says. "All hospitals have that same smell!"

Returning to the surgical waiting room, Don, Harriet, and Brian, are exactly where I left them a few hours earlier.

"They took her into surgery," I inform them.

"How is she doing?" asks Harriet, looking up from her knitting. Harriet is Debbie's stepmother.

"She is a little nervous," I say, and wince to convey understatement. "They will give her something to take the edge off."

"Oh, God bless her," says Harriet with an empathetic shake of her head.

The large room is packed to capacity. Many are passing time reading. In addition to Harriet, a few other women are knitting. At one table, a board game is underway, and at another is a picture puzzle. Some sit or stand, eyes looking at nothing in particular—minds focused on concerns, I expect.

Feeling a need to get away for a while, I say, "Dad, Debbie gave me strict orders to take you for a walk."

"That's our Debbie," says Harriet.

We all smile.

"Sounds good to me," Don replies with real interest.

"Who else wants to go?" I query.

"I do," chimes Brian.

"How about you, Harriet?" I ask.

"No way!" Harriet tightens her sweater around herself, and shudders at the thought of the chill. "I'm staying here where it's warm while you boys are out there freezing."

We all chuckle.

Confident of a long vigil, the three of us bundle up, and set out for downtown Iowa City. Our route takes us out the hospital's back entrance.

"Damn, it's cold," I say.

Zero degrees Fahrenheit, but the morning sun is shining bright, and there's very little wind for March in Iowa.

Heading for their day's first lecture, a tight-packed torrent of college students carries us along as if we are whitewater rafting. Sameness of heavy-hooded coats and backpacks masks their gender. Walking single-file with the flow, staying canoe-close to keep from getting separated, we navigate our way across University of Iowa's campus. Sharp ridges of ice defining the edges of hard-packed snowbanks along the walkways are evidence of an odd few days when temperatures rose above freezing. Crossing a bridge, we look down into the roiling surge of the Iowa River.

"Would sure hate to fall in there," I say.

Making the east bank, Hawkeye scholars course around us as we pause to take in the old state capitol's gold dome glistening against a crisp blue sky.

"Beautiful," Don says.

It's hard to be in the moment mentally. My thoughts are with Debbie. Hard to believe we've been married for nineteen years. The exercise, fresh air, and scenery have numbed my anxieties a bit. Feeling powerless, I think of the four-hour procedure she is undergoing. Dr. Martin has been a godsend since our move to Iowa three years ago. She is confident that the removal of thirty percent of Debbie's liver will resolve our current predicament. I take comfort in that thought.

"Let's walk downtown. That way," I point in a two o'clock direction.

The cold is biting hard so we limit our exploration of the area to a quick glance down one of the streets permanently closed to vehicular traffic. Restaurants and shops, primarily appealing to students and visiting parents, line the way.

"The city turned this section of town into a Ped-Mall a few years ago," I report.

"What's a 'ped'?" asks Brian.

"Ped's short for pedestrian," I answer.

"Ohhh," Brian says with an I-should-have-figured-that-out grin.

"We'd better head back," I say. "Don't want to be gone too long."

"My feet are getting frosty," says Don.

"I should have brought along a carrot for your nose; maybe some coal for your eyes, and mouth, plus a black top hat," I joke. "All of the children would play with you. I'm thinking there might be a song in it, *Donald, the Snowman*."

"Always a joker. Brian, don't take after your dad, okay?"

Our return path leads us to the hospital's main entrance. We turn a corner lined by a high wooden fence enclosing a new medical wing under construction.

"There it is, Iowa's cathedral to college football, Kinnick Stadium! You can see down onto the field from on top of that parking garage," I say, pointing up at one of the three multi-level garages positioned between the stadium and the massive medical center.

"Getting to this hospital on a game day is quite an adventure. Iowans love their Hawkeyes."

Leading the way into the hospital through a plywood maze of construction corridors, I find the correct set of elevators. We exit at the appropriate floor, and stride into the surgical waiting room, somewhat out of breath. The lingering benefits from our walk are melted by the reception. Harriet and Deb Tarara, Dr. Martin's assistant, are standing in front of the information desk. Deb Tarara is on the phone with her back to us.

Harriet, on lookout, says, "Oh, look, they're here!", and taps Deb's arm without taking her eyes off us.

Deb Tarara turns, and her mouth drops open with surprised relief.

To the person on the phone she says, "Never mind, thank God, they just walked in."

She hangs up the receiver.

"Wow! Am I ever glad to see you! Why did you leave the hospital?" she scolds. "I was organizing a search party."

Next to her, Harriet, now in tears, says, "I didn't know what to do. I didn't know how to find you."

Alarmed, I ask, "Is Debbie okay?"

"Yes, but Dr. Martin needs to speak with you right away," Deb says with a raw edge of urgency.

While being ushered into "Family Conference Room Number Two," I resist the urge to panic by moving my thoughts to a protected mental compartment. As a naval officer, the ability to compartmentalize serves me well during stressful shipboard maneuvers, engineering casualties, fires, flooding, and actual combat conditions. To function in battle mode at the eye of any storm, I endeavor to live by the Kipling mantra "...keep your head while all about you are losing theirs."

The room is small, but comfortable. It resembles a compact living room with pleasant paintings. A plush floral love seat against the far wall is flanked by lamps on end tables and matching armchairs. The four of us fill the available seats. Dr. Martin enters, exuding energy as if she too has been on a brisk walk. She is a full-figured woman with a cheerful face and commanding presence. Her white lab coat has a just-thrown-on appearance with part of the collar tucked under, and the unbuttoned front reveals green scrubs. "Maureen Martin, M.D." is embroidered above the left pocket. Her hair is veiled by the same type of blue disposable hair cover Debbie was donning this morning.

This woman oversees the organ transplant program at University of Iowa Medical Center, and has been the only doctor with hope and solutions for Debbie's survival. Debbie and I have come to like and respect her, immensely. She is, in our experience, a rare type of doctor—a true "think outside the box" problem solver and risk taker. A bit of a maverick.

"Well, we found you. Deb Tarara was about to pull her hair out! Hello, everyone," she beams with good natured confidence.

Standing up, I receive her firm handshake, and reintroduce my family. Deb Tarara arrives pushing two chairs on rollers. We all sit down.

Dr. Martin begins, punctuating comments with her hands.

"First, Debbie is fine. Her vital signs are all good. She is sedated, and my medical team is taking magnificent care of her.

"Chuck, it's good you have your family here today. We have an important decision to make, and very little time. To be blunt, the cancer is much more widespread than scans revealed."

Battening my mental hatches, I steer into the storm of facts being presented. Maureen stands up, and erases a detailed hand-drawing of a heart from a whiteboard mounted on the sidewall. Leftover from a previous family conference, a ghost-like outline of the heart remains visible. How did that surgery turn out, I wonder? Did the patient survive? How did that family handle the situation?

Dr. Martin chooses from a variety of colored dry erase markers lying end-to-end along the bottom ledge of the whiteboard. She draws a rough sketch of a normal liver with its eight lobes in brown, and the eight blood supplies in red. The acrid smell of dry erase markers fills the room, making everyone wince.

"Ooh," Harriet squints, and pinches her nose between her thumb and forefinger.

"Sorry about the smell of the markers, Harriet," says Dr. Martin. "You'll get used to it in a minute."

Then, in black, she darkens the massive areas of tumor she had discovered during her examination.

"I held Debbie's liver just like this," she says.

Holding her hands out in front of her as if gripping an invisible liver, her studied fingers reenact the scene, adjusting to unseen contours, and applying evaluative pressure to suspect areas. Describing the use of ultrasound to expose the organ's secrets, she continues the pantomime.

Concluding, Maureen states, "The situation is, to completely remove the cancer, we would have to excise seven of the eight lobes of Debbie's liver. In this case, that comprises approximately ninety percent of the organ because the only lobe that does not appear to contain tumors is very small."

"Why didn't the scans show the extent of this cancer?" asks my father-in-law.

"Don, scans are great tools, but the technology is not yet perfected. Someday, we will know exactly what is going on inside our bodies. Unfortunately, we're not there yet—we still have to discover the truth with surgery."

Debbie and I are already familiar with the limitations of scans. This is Debbie's second liver surgery performed by Dr. Martin. The first time, scans had shown what appeared to be a cluster of tumors. During surgery, that area turned out to be noncancerous scar tissue. Fortunately, by some fluke, an actual adrenal tumor was discovered, and removed where none had been detected by scans.

"Ninety percent! How is that even possible?" asks Don.

"Luckily," Maureen responds, "we can survive for a while with just ten percent of our liver."

"So, this operation would *really* push the envelope," I say.

Dr. Martin pauses for a moment of introspection, and then continues, "Under normal circumstances, I would not even suggest such a drastic operation; the chances of survival are very slim, but I know Debbie. She is strong. She is a fighter. In fact, she is remarkably healthy for someone with such an extensive cancer history."

We all nod in agreement.

In the nine years since her first diagnosis, Debbie has amazed everyone.

"Looking at her, you would never know there is anything wrong. She looks so healthy!" people say upon hearing her history.

To this point in time, Debbie has suffered the removal of her left adrenal gland, left kidney, spleen, and the removal, and reconstruction of both breasts. She has undergone a multitude of radiation treatments, and six months of chemotherapy. Also, metastatic adrenal tumors, having spread from the original adrenal cancer, have been removed from her right lung and liver. She has survived an astounding four primary cancers, including two independent breast cancers, adrenal cancer, and a malignant fibrous histiocytoma (MFH). MFH sometimes occurs as an unfortunate side effect of the radiation used to combat cancer.

Even her doctors are in awe.

Describing her, one rather geeky oncologist commented, "Statistically speaking, she is conspicuously thriving in the extreme righthand tail of several overlapping cancer survival probability bell curves. She is so many standard deviations from the statistical norm, her being alive is a highly curious anomaly."

Yes, she is a fascinating patient.

Dr. Martin taps on the appropriate part of her drawing with the capped end of a dry erase marker.

"For some reason, this one little lobe of Debbie's liver has been sitting there doing almost nothing for her entire life. I think it explains why it is the only one out of eight lobes without any tumors. I believe it is just big enough to do the job. If we are lucky, she could be cancer free."

Maureen pulls her chair up close to us, and sits down.

"The liver is the only organ that regenerates. Over the next six to nine months, that little piece," she says, pointing back at the whiteboard, "can regrow to the size of a normal liver. However, it will always be a single lobe with only one blood supply.

"Time is short. You have three options. One, we close her up; you go home, and enjoy life as long as possible."

The scenario plays out in my mind. My stomach constricts.

"The second option: we close, wait for her to wake up, and ask what she wants to do. Third, we remove the seven lobes we know have active tumors now, but...and you need to fully understand what I am about to tell you...if we do this operation, and it doesn't work, Debbie will be in a coma within three days, and dead within a week. I'm sorry to be so blunt, but it is imperative you are completely aware of what we are facing."

She pauses to allow us to get our minds around the dilemma.

I immediately dismiss the second course of action as cowardly. I know how Debbie would have decided this question had she known these facts prior to surgery—she would have gone for it. However, if we go with option two and wake her up for a decision, I fear she will not be in a state of mind to make a rational choice—she will say no. It is my duty to make this decision on her behalf. After nineteen years of marriage, nearly half of that time battling cancer with her, I am up to it.

"I believe we should remove the tumor now, but this is a life-and-death decision. I want to hear what everyone else thinks," I say.

"Would a transplant be possible?" asks Don.

"We seriously considered the transplant option a few years ago, and for various reasons did not go down that road. Unfortunately, at this point, Debbie's cancer is far too advanced for a transplant."

"What are the odds this surgery will work?" Harriet asks.

"Look, the odds are not very good, not good at all, Harriet," Dr. Martin says with an edge. "The problem with the odds is they don't take the individual into account. Each person and what they are capable of handling is different. We know what the odds are if we do nothing—she will die in a matter of months. If we close her up, you will at least have those months with her."

Maureen pauses to reflect.

"I know Debbie," she continues. "My gut tells me she can survive this surgery. Possibly even come out of it cancer free, and live a long normal life.

"She has told me many times how much she wants to be around to raise her two sons."

She looks at my son, Brian, with a melancholy smile.

"I also know she has a strong support team," she says, and gestures to all of us with open palms. "Your encouragement will be essential to her recovery, if you decide to go ahead with this surgery."

Searching our faces, she says, "I know this is a lot to take in, and it is a difficult decision, but right now Debbie is on the operating table with her insides hanging out waiting for us to make up our minds."

Looking directly at me, she asks, "What are you going to do, Chuck?"

Nine years of constant guerrilla warfare with cancer has prepared me for this moment. My knees are not going to buckle under the weight of this decision. Our battles have turned Debbie and me into a well-tested team. We are changed: much braver, stronger, and more determined than when cancer first entered our lives. We have grown in faith, love, and understanding of how we should live, and how we should face our adversary—cancer. We know the disease may one day beat us, but we have agreed to never accept defeat. I am prepared for this decision with a foundational philosophy of life.

Resolute, I respond, "Like you, Dr. Martin, I know Debbie. I know her mind. We have an agreement to never allow cancer to be in the driver seat. She would want this surgery. Removing these tumors is the only option we can live with. She needs to be around to see her grandkids."

I look to my father-in-law for a reaction. He mirrors aspects of Debbie's looks and mannerisms. His intense concentration is obvious in the squint of his left eye, set of his jaw, pursed lips, and piercing focus on a point of fact in his mind.

Nodding his head, he looks at me, and points as he says, "This is your decision, Chuck, but I want you to know I agree."

He taps a knuckle against his chin.

"Debbie has always been a fighter," he says with pride, and then continues with an element of anger in his voice, "Three years ago, we drove out here from New York to be with her after her first doctor at this very hospital sent her home to get her affairs in order."

He pauses, and in a much kinder tone, "Dr. Martin, she would not be alive today if not for you."

Looking around at all of us, he states, "If there is a real chance Debbie might live cancer-free, we have to take it! I think God still has a purpose for her. Everyone back home says she is a miracle!"

"I think she's an angel!" blurts Harriet, unable to restrain herself any longer. "She has survived so much, and helped so many people. Everybody calls *her* when they are facing cancer!"

Up to this point, Harriet sat stone quiet with her fist tightly frozen to her lips. Only her eyes had moved, shifting quickly from one to the other of us as we spoke.

Dr. Martin looks at my son, smiles, and asks gently, "What do you think, Brian?"

Quietly taking everything in, Brian, except for his blond hair and blue eyes, is another reflection of his mother.

Without delay, and with a certainty and composed defiance that makes me ever so proud, Brian responds, "My mom would not want to live sick. She would want this surgery."

Dr. Martin smiles, and looks at Brian with admiration.

"We're in agreement then. Like you, Brian, that little piece of liver is going to grow up fast and do what we ask of it," she concludes, and stands up.

"Now, in the days ahead, if her liver should start to wobble," she says with a grin, and a twinkle in her eye, "I have a few tricks up my sleeve to keep her going."

Taking a last look at us, she says, "I will see all of you after this operation," and strides out with purpose.

Deb Tarara remains behind.

"You are welcome to stay in this room for as long as you need it. That telephone," she says, pointing to one on an end table, "is there for your use. Call anyone you need to call." She touches my arm, looks into my eyes, and assures me, "You made the right decision."

She closes the door behind her, leaving the four of us alone. The mission we had been built for is complete. We have made the most difficult decision of our lives. Like a ship assigned to draw enemy fire while supporting the landing of troops on a heavily defended beach, we spent ourselves absorbing direct hits. Damaged beyond saving, we break up, and sink. Down we go, all crying convulsively, and bracing each other for collision with the bottom.

My mind replays recent calls of *support* from well-meaning relatives. One salty individual warned me, "Be prepared. Once cancer gets in their liver, it's over. If they ever give *me* that news, I'll *shoot* myself before it gets too bad."

My mother asked me point blank, "Where are you planning to bury Debbie? There in Iowa or will you bring her back home to New York to be near her family?"

I want so much for them to be wrong. I want the decision I just made to prove them wrong.

Part of me has been mourning the death of my wife for many years. A sea of depression and simmering anger ebbs and flows with the pull of grief that accompanies each cancer diagnosis. I don't know how I *should* feel when cancer returns, again and again, but I *know* how to be angry, and at times I boil over. Also at play are emotional vestiges of my childhood. In reaction to family turmoil in my youth, I chose disconnection and emotional numbness. Closing my core-self behind a door in my heart was how I escaped the world. There, in my private hell, I grew up stewing in pressing disappointment with my parents, and anger with God. That door continues to separate me from true and complete trusting, caring, and loving.

The love I feel for my wife remains on my terms, a product, as I perceive it, of my own will. My protective door is very much at odds with a promise I made to myself. In reaction to the gut-wrenching breakup of my parent's marriage, I swore never to do the same thing to my children. As an idealistic youth, I dedicated myself to permanence in marriage. Staying in a relationship through thick and thin is foundational to parenthood for me. Having suffered from promises broken, I determined to keep the vows I would make on *my* wedding day—no matter what! Further, I set for myself an expectation that I would achieve a visionary level of love and relationship in *my* marriage.

The reality that permanence is God's intention for marriage, and that only through God is infinite love available, was not part of my teenage world of thought. In fact, from my early teens until I was thirty-five, I referred to myself as a devout agnostic. While I was busy doubting his existence, God was at work using the bad examples in my life to teach me fundamental lessons of good.

These past few years, as I have been rebuilding my relationship with God, his love has been seeping into my heart, flooding my secret room, like water into a basement. I was not expecting to confront my long-locked mental door here in "Family Conference Room Number Two," but here it is. This is my chance to escape from myself. If I remain here, in this cell of refuge, I will surely die. I have never been so afraid in my life. The pain I am experiencing is breaking out into the room through my tears and sobbing moans. My refuge has become a place of crushing fear and unbearable pain. It's time for a decision. It's time to acknowledge, and open myself to life as I want to experience it. Removing the barricades and inner locks, I am choosing to kick my door wide open. I am changed. My decision allows profound feelings to finally reach me. A complete awareness of the depth of my love for Debbie overtakes me— infinitely greater than I could ever realize on my own terms.

Finally, I am free to feel, care, trust, and love purely. More powerful than my wildest dreams, it's as if I have come ashore in a place I feared to be only legend. Climbing to a windswept pinnacle with a commanding view, I plant the flag of my soul. I have discovered the land of unbounded love. A real place idealized over the ages in songs, poetry, stories, and letters of affection; a territory accessible only through God. I claim residency in this kingdom. I am home!

But with the unfiltered experience of feelings, thoughts of losing Debbie within the next seven days become impossible to bear. The most powerful wave of despair I have ever encountered rolls over me. I choke on anguish as, again and again, I relive the decision to authorize the surgery. Did I just make the biggest mistake of my life? Debbie might be dead within seven days because of my decision to go ahead with the surgery. Am I losing months with her based on false hope of having a lifetime? Did I make my decision out of pride? The next three days could be my last chance to communicate with her in this life. What will I say to her? What if she dies? Have I killed her? What of our two sons—what will it be like for *them* to grow up without a mother? How will *I* ever go on without *her* as my wife?

My strength fails me. Giving up, I plead, "God, I can't do this! Please help me! Please help me!"

As if from someone seated beside me in the gloom, I clearly hear from within me a perfect and wholly calm voice say, "Have faith."

I am stunned. What has just happened? How can this be? Did God just speak to me? Actually speak to me? To *me*! Every part of me knows he did, and tingles and reverberates with the meaning of God's words of comfort to me. I have no doubt. Joy overcomes panic, and I breathe deep knowing Debbie will survive this episode as she has so many others.

"Debbie will be okay. Have faith," I repeat to myself. "Have faith!"

How will I live knowing, without reservation, that God is real, and involved in my life? I don't know why God chose to speak to me, but I do know the creator of the universe loves me.

My eyes have been clamped shut for I don't know how long. Opening them, I look around at the others. Everyone has similarly recovered, and returned to the surface. Their heads bob up and down as if floating on their thoughts. How loud was I? Did I cry out?

Despite personal certainty that my wife will survive, I instinctively know it is important for Debbie's survival to see other members of her family and some close friends in the coming days.

"We had better call everyone, and tell them to come on the run in case she slips into a coma," I say.

We call her mother, sister, brothers, various other friends, and relatives. Taking turns on the phone, we listen to and learn from each other how to more quickly share the important details of Debbie's situation, and make clear their need to get here quick. Hours pass. The surgery is completed. Debbie transitions from the recovery room to intensive care. In the evening, local Iowa friends come to see her. The next day, people pour in from New York, Colorado, Kansas, and Florida.

Through weeks of sleeping on chairs, and waiting room floors, God gives me strength and peace.

One day a devout and dear Christian friend, Correne Hendricksen, comes for a visit. My serenity and good spirits surprise her. She begins to cry.

I hold her, and say, "Debbie's going to be fine."

In tears, she looks up at me, and admits, "I cried my entire drive over from Davenport. I was certain Debbie is not going to make it this time. I don't understand—I came here to comfort you, but instead, you are comforting me. How is it you are so confident, so...at peace?"

"I am at peace," I say. "God spoke to me, and told me that Debbie is going to be fine."

She hugs me, and sobs. Correne is one of the most God-centered and spiritual people I have ever met. My revelation comes as no surprise to her, but as welcome news. She does not doubt what I told her—not even a little bit.

Maybe someday I will be ready to tell others, but right now, I am going to keep my message from God to myself.

# CHAPTER 8

# WAKING UP

*(Debbie)*

Awakening from anesthetic sleep following major surgery is a surreal process I have experienced far too many times. As the drugs release their dark hold, my imagination interprets the return to awareness with a recurring vision. Floating over and through dense fog and clouds, I am suspended beneath a hot air balloon. Content, reposed in my basket, free of worldly concerns, my perception of time ebbs and flows. Mere moments are confused with extended periods. Questions of how long I have been drifting take shape and tumble among my thoughts. In due course, I grasp that my balloon is tethered from far below, and being hauled hand-over-unseen-hand toward the ground. Whispers climb into my dream on the edges of echoes. A protest grows within me. I don't want to go back—I dread the pain waiting for me.

The low rumblings of distant storms draw near. Beeps and whirs of medical machinery, and the murmurings of my family separate, and bit by bit words become distinguishable.

My mind is spinning as I descend...down, down. The knowledge of what to expect, fear, and regret builds as I return to earth. The thud of pain is as abrupt as Dorothy's arrival in Oz. Landing in a bright narrow valley, each breath delivers hurt. Low voices of the mountainous shapes towering either side of me grow familiar...my husband...my father...my stepmother. One peak remains silent. Slighter than the others, I know it to be my oldest son, Brian.

"She's coming around."

"I hope she doesn't get sick this time."

"Get the nurse."

An automatic blood pressure cuff constricts my upper right arm to the point of discomfort. I hold my breath until...satisfied, it releases with a sigh. A rhythm opens itself up to me, a sort of "medical jazz." The intermittent grip on my arm, and strum of inflatable stockings squeezing my legs to prevent blood clots support an orchestra of medical equipment. Voices of my family join, at times, the beeps and whirs and pulsing backbeat of a heart monitor.

My sense of smell clicks on. The distinct odors of Betadine and sterilized hospital linens trigger the first stage of nausea. The balloon-basket has transformed into a hospital bed surrounded by people who love me. The fog of my dream is gone, but my sight is distorted by a thick veil of glycerin placed there to keep my eyes from drying out. Time to begin my reorientation checklist.

Where...when am I? Why am I here?

Trying to look around to get my bearings, the weight of my head is beyond my strength. Room is shaped like a wedge of pie after a few forkfuls have been eaten from the pointy end. Nope, I've never been here before.

Surgery...I had surgery on my liver, I recall, and blink, blink, blink to clear the petroleum-jelly like goop from my eyes. Centered in my view, held to the textured white ceiling tiles by colored pushpins, is the picture-poster of a colorful hot-air balloon rising across a rainbow. Rainbow—God's promise.

Movement in my peripheral view is of people aware of my return. Breathing is difficult – hurts like hell.

An authoritative woman's voice says, "Family, I must ask you to step out of the room for a few minutes? I'll bring you back as soon as I check her vitals and get her situated. Sorry, these I.C.U. cubicles are not designed for crowds."

My mind replays what I heard, confused by the term "I.C.U." The letters tumble over and over. Click...click...click, ah, I am in the Intensive Care Unit.

The face of a nurse enters my blurred field of vision. I blink to focus.

"Mrs. Wilson, my name is Sarah. I'll be taking care of you this evening. Do you know where you are?"

I consider the question...where am I? I just answered that one. Where...?

"...I.C.U.?" I manage to mumble.

"I see you, too," she jokes.

I like her immediately.

"Your surgery is over, and *yes*, you are in *my* I.C.U. I will take *very* good care of you. How's your pain level?"

I answer by purposefully widening and bulging out my eyes.

"That bad, huh? Okay, on a scale of zero to ten, with zero being no pain and ten being the worst you can imagine, how would you rate the intensity?"

"Twenty," I respond with lips barely able to form intelligible words.

"Reeeally bad," she interprets with a knowing smile.

"My throat hurts....I'm going to throw up," I warn.

"Unfortunately, your throat is irritated from the breathing tube they inserted during surgery. It will feel raw and scratchy for a day or two, but it's nothing to worry about. I'm going to put some medicine in your I.V., something to control your nausea, and hopefully relieve your pain."

Picking up my hand, she places two of her fingers in my palm.

"Squeeze as hard as you can."

I constrict firmly.

"Good. Now, I want to see you move your legs."

I shuffle my legs slightly; pain rips through my abdomen.

"Excellent!" she says, a consummate cheerleader.

"Your family is right outside the door. I'll bring them in shortly, but first I want to make you as comfortable as possible. I'm going to raise your head a little," she informs me as she feels for a button on the bed's side rail.

The bed and I both groan as the upper half of my body angles upward; shots of pain throb through my midsection. The lever motion pulls the loosely tied hospital gown off my shoulder.

"*Owwwhhhh*," I moan. "I hurt."

Every word is an exertion. It even hurts to complain.

"I'm freezing," I shiver.

"Here, let me tie up your gown and get you a blanket."

She adjusts my gown, and disappears briefly, returning with a warmed blanket and extra pillows.

"You might be more comfortable if I position a pillow on either side of you."

Preparing for the pain I know is coming, I hold my breath as she first rolls me slightly to the right, and then back to the left, leaving me sandwiched between two pillows.

"Is that better?" she asks, hopefully.

"I don't know," I reply as I exhale the breath I held through the ordeal.

The elevated position has brought my family into view. They are watching me through a glass wall a few feet beyond the foot of my bed. A wave of relief washes over me upon seeing them close by. Pleading with my eyes, I will them into the room. As if reading my thoughts, the nurse motions them in.

"Family, I need your help with something very important. I am going to show our patient how to use this gadget to clear her lungs. You need to encourage her to use it often; at the least, every half hour. She's not going to like it, but it's critical to her recovery that she expand her lungs frequently. Otherwise she's at risk of developing pneumonia."

Turning to me, Nurse Sarah presents a small handheld apparatus with two side-by-side clear plastic tubular sections. A flexible blue hose with a mouthpiece on one end protrudes from the center of the device.

86

One cylinder is demarked by a graduated scale, and contains a little yellow ball. There is an adjustable red arrow beside it.

"Mrs. Wilson, this is an incentive spirometer. Through this mouthpiece, I want you to inhale as much air as you can. Your goal is to move the yellow float up toward the goal marker." She points out the red arrow, and slides it up and down in its track. "Count to ten as you inhale, keeping the float aloft as long as you can. This helps us measure the volume of air you are taking in. We will raise this goal marker as your lungs get stronger."

To me, this training session is like a seatbelt and air mask demonstration to a frequent flyer. I have a stockpile of incentive spirometers— souvenirs from my many surgeries. She positions the mouthpiece close to my lips.

"I can't," I resist.

"You have to try," she insists.

Reluctant, I allow the mechanism into my mouth, and make a feeble attempt to inhale. The resulting cough sends pain searing through my body.

"Good job. Again," she chirps like a fitness coach.

Turning my head away, I hope she will leave me alone. Instead, she hands me a pillow, advising me to hug it to my stomach. Taking another breath, I clutch the pillow tight to my abdomen through the ensuing coughing episode.

The nurse smiles, "Okay, that's a pretty good start, but you have to keep it up—it's extremely important."

"I'll try," I mumble.

"No, you *have* to do it …often! Do you understand?" she emphasizes with a surprising burst of drama.

"Yes, okay, I'll do it," I promise, lying.

Somehow, I know that she knows I am willing to say anything to make her stop.

"I'm going to leave you with your family now, but first I want to show you the call button. Don't hesitate to use it. If you need anything, I'll be right in."

She breezes out of the room.

My husband moves close to the bed, grasps my hand in his, and leans over the bedrail so we are face-to-face. Looking into my eyes, he says, "I love you, honey."

"How did it go?" I whisper hoarsely. "Has Dr. Martin told you anything yet?"

"Dr. Martin told us the operation went quite well."

"But what did she say? What did she tell you?" I persist.

"She said she would be in to give us more details after you wake up."

"Did she get all of the cancer out?"

"Yes, she was able to remove all of the cancer."

Chuck steps back to allow room for my father.

"Hi Dad," I manage, as he grasps my hand.

"How are you doing, honey?"

"I hurt all over," I say. "Did Chuck take you for a walk?"

"Yes, we went for a nice walk," he responds.

Again, to him, "Have you seen Dr. Martin?"

"Yes, she came out, and spoke to us for a few minutes after the surgery, and told us everything went well."

I repeat my previous question, "Did she say whether she was able to get all of the cancer out?"

"She's quite sure she got all the cancer."

"Where's Brian?"

Dad and Chuck make a space for Brian to step into my view between them. Facial features of the men either side of him reflect in his.

"Hi Mama," he says sweetly.

My oldest son takes my hand.

"Hi Bri," I say as I connect with him. Discovering his fingers in mine, I squeeze them. I can't help being happy, looking at his handsome young face, blue eyes, and blondish hair. My memory does a quick rewind, and

I recall his development from an infant in my arms to a towheaded toddler; his years playing baseball, trombone, and computer games. Always a great comfort to me, especially during the long months of his father's overseas deployments.

Somehow, he has matured since this morning. His eyes are carrying a different set of concerns since I last saw him—much heavier. In fact, I detect the presence of a huge weight bearing down on everyone.

"Where's Harriet?" I ask.

"I'm right here, honey," she answers from the doorway.

"You must be worn out," I say to her.

"Don't worry, I'm doing fine," she assures me.

Throughout the afternoon, I fade in and out of consciousness. Each time I awaken, the blue tube is wagged in my face by a well-meaning family member. Sucking in air, the little yellow ball hovers upward to the target level. While I cough, my cheering section reacts, "Good job... way to go...keep it up."

A peculiar level of attentiveness to my every waking moment, combined with infinite niceness, mild evasiveness, and a hint of feigned innocence, causes me to become suspicious. This act is familiar. It's obvious my family has not told me everything about my medical situation. With each awakening, I try again to break through their collusion, but they stand firm. Dr. Martin must come before I will know what is really going on. Resigning myself to waiting, my eyes become heavy. I drift off—a relief for my family, I'm sure.

My husband gently recalls me to consciousness, "Debbie, Dr. Martin is here." Opening my eyes, I am relieved to see Dr. Maureen Martin's reassuring smile. She is accompanied by her assistant, Deb Tarara. These two people are both larger than life to me. They are a life-saving answer to prayer. Without their appearance in my life a few years ago, I would almost certainly be dead.

"How's our girl doing?" asks Maureen.

"I hurt," I manage to say.

Struggling to keep my eyes open, I begin to question her.

"How did it go?"

She crosses the room smiling, leans close, takes my hand, and beams her strength into my face.

"Well, it should come as no surprise," she begins with a twinkle in her eye, "but it turns out the situation with your liver was even more complicated than expected."

Realizing I am about to hear some challenging news, my nerves tingle despite the pain medications. I hurt everywhere.

"Were you able to remove the entire tumor?" I ask.

"Yes, but, I had to remove much more of your liver than originally intended."

My mind is in overdrive, but my imagination is at a loss as to what I am about to hear. Holding my breath, I know my life has changed tracks.

She continues with confidence, "Debbie, during surgery this morning I discovered adrenal tumors were actively involved in seven of the eight lobes of your liver. I left the operating room, and held a meeting with your family. Let me assure you, we discussed the specifics of your situation in detail, and examined all options thoroughly. Together, we determined the only acceptable option was the one that offered you the chance of long-term survival. We decided to remove those seven cancerous lobes, which as it turned out, comprised at least ninety percent of your liver. The remaining lobe is so small because it has sort of been on the dole, just along for the ride, all these years. The other lobes have been doing all the work, which is why they contain the tumors. Lucky for you, this little piece," she holds her hand in front of her face, and focuses her eyes on the approximate two-inch space between her thumb and index finger, "appears healthy, and cancer-free. However, it may be a lazy cuss, and not much appreciate being put to work after all these years goofing off," she says with her characteristic twinkle.

If I were fully conscious I would be shocked. The pain medication and after-effects of anesthesia dampen the impact. Like any good leader, Dr. Martin has worked herself up to a point at which she embodies vision, and shares a bounty of confidence. However, I notice the hopeful look on Deb Tarara's face is the result of great effort on her part to overcome doubt. Further, I sense everyone in the room is struggling both to convince themselves—as well as me—everything is going to be okay. Comprehending that I have undergone something extraordinary, I center my emotions and attention on Dr. Martin's self-assured nature. Calming myself, I buy what she is selling—at full-price.

"We made the best possible decision," she continues. "However, we're not out of the woods."

Closing my eyes, I attempt to shut out the world.

"You are in for a rough couple of days while your body responds to this major insult. We need ten percent of our liver to survive, but that lazy little bit of liver now has to perform the load of chores your entire hard-working organ used to share."

Envisioning the new arrangement of organs in my abdomen, I struggle to come to grips with the idea ninety percent of my liver is gone.

"Am I going to survive?"

"We have some serious challenges ahead of us."

She looks directly into my eyes, "Debbie, I have to tell you, there is a significant chance this won't work. You are in an extremely serious situation. I would not have performed this surgery on just anybody. I know you as a person. I am well aware of your fighting spirit. You," she says pointing at me, "are fully capable of making it through this challenge. You will need lots of support from everyone in this room, and many others but," her words soar, "within six to nine months, that tiny single lobe will grow to the size of a normal liver. It's a miracle organ, and you are a miracle woman."

With this last statement, her hands which were held out in front of her shake, and seem to be holding an unseen something the size of a large meatloaf. The immensity of the situation continues to take shape in my mind. The question wells up, again.

"Am I going to die?"

Taking my hand, she responds gently, "You are very unwell right now, Debbie, but I have a few tricks up my sleeve to keep you going if what's left of your liver should start to wobble. The fact is, you are in great danger. You need all the love and support you can get. Your close family members should be called in. Their presence will encourage your recovery."

"We've already called them," Chuck interjects.

Thoughts of my mother, my sister, my brothers, other beloved friends and family members flash through my mind. I have undergone many surgeries, but my family has never been called in. Thoughts of dying, and leaving these individuals behind terrify me. Closing my eyes, I attempt to shut out the world, and allow the fog of my pain medications to roll in.

When the going gets tough, I often experience droughts of faith, what I call "desert times" or periods of severe doubt or disagreement with God. Embarrassment stems from the fact that, having survived so many battles with cancer, people expect me to cheerfully rise to the challenge each time a new tumor lights up a scan. They tell me I'm brave and strong—after all, I have two "Courage Awards" from The American Cancer Society to prove it—but even I grow weary of my saga. Admitting such qualms used to feel like an unappreciative affront to God.

Due to my battle scars and longevity I am often presented to friends of friends, at least those who have received a recent cancer diagnosis, as a "go-to" resource with a "wow!" reputation. Motivated by both a sense of responsibility and base pride, I do my best to hearten these freshman cancer warriors. Often, when lured into believing my own press, I get frustrated coming up short in my role as a super-human bastion of faith. Considering my inexplicable endurance, I am particularly ashamed of my inadequacies and chronic ingratitude. The hardest part is to *not* act "the part" but be comfortable in my own skin—share the truth of my experience, warts and all.

At some point in the middle of whatever my latest cancer crisis happens to be, I settle down and take the time to regain perspective. Once I hand the overwhelming burden over to God, I can discern—from a place beyond reason—he chose to reveal evidence of his existence through me. I also recall I promised to do anything for him in return. Sometimes, I slip into misunderstanding my purpose, and reason that he expects me to always share my story with a shiny, seamless, smiley, and spotlessly-positive attitude. The truth is, sometimes being positive is beyond the strength available to me. That's when Chuck and others remind me I am not in this on my own. Why is it that, after all I have been through, I still need reminding?

For much of my life, I was not ready to believe in God. Faith is an intimately personal decision that for me was dormant, existing only as a tiny seed secretly shielded since youth. Never did I expect to need faith, but when I did, it blossomed into a shade-giving plant that leaves in its season. When it's in bloom, I live comfortably in its shade. When it's not, I cling to its remnant. The faith component of my story makes sense only when people are ready to hear it. Regarding faith, Chuck always says: "You can only see it when you 'see' it." Like a math problem, it's nonsense until understanding dawns.

Even among people of faith, reactions to my promise story are mixed. Some find their beliefs invigorated. Others listen through clenched smiles, sympathetically reasoning that if they were dying of cancer, even they might be susceptible to latching onto a similarly flimsy excuse for hope. My story is interesting to all, but dismissed by most as useful madness that allows me to keep fighting. I can't blame them. After all, my optimism was based on a lucky shot as I poked my finger into a Bible during a fit of angst. How ridiculous! Logic continues to yell uncertainties in my head, but the promise has deep roots, intertwined with the faith I need to believe—belief beyond reason.

# CHAPTER 9

# OF WEDDINGS, BIRTHDAYS, AND BREASTS

### *(Debbie)*

"I had a dream last night I still had real breasts with real nipples reacting to touch and to cold," I say.

"Oh yeah," Chuck says, and goes silent.

It's my birthday. I'm fifty-three.

Three years ago, in 2006, for my fiftieth, Chuck took me on a cruise to the Bahamas and tried to surprise me by arranging for our Iowa friends (Rick & Susan Stacy, Ron & Mardi Burmeister and Tom & Lynda Gerhardt—only the Burmeisters still live in Iowa) to meet us on the ship. Inadvertently, I discovered what Chuck was up to. I tried to act like I did not know about his scheme, but had to fess up. It was a wonderful gesture and we all had a great time.

Anyway, this year, Chuck and I are sitting next to Rick and Susan Stacy's pool behind their home near Marble Falls, Texas. Chuck resigned from a position as a financial advisor with Merrill Lynch in Bonita Springs, Florida about six months ago, after three years in the business. He decided it was not what he wanted to spend his life doing and has been focusing on writing and taking care of me. My mother passed away last year which was the most difficult loss of my life. I cried for weeks, could not sleep and my health was in jeopardy as another cancer made itself known. Another breast cancer, discovered under my right arm. There was a small bit of breast tissue remaining from my long-ago breast removal, just enough for a third primary breast cancer to take hold. I got the news at my mother's funeral reception.

Following the marriages of our sons—Brian's was before my mom's death and Greg's was after—we began to consider what to do next, where to move to. My health was relatively stable, for me, and being used to moving every few years, it seemed only natural that a new chapter begin in a new location. The idea of moving north, closer to the bulk of our extended family, began to take shape. Then, my sister moved from her position as President of the Bonita Springs Chamber of Commerce to a faraway chamber in Pennsylvania. Having lived for a few years within a mile of Nancy and her husband, Chris, the prospect of remaining in Florida without her nearby did not appeal to me.

The reason we moved to Florida from Tennessee in the first place was to be near family for help "at the end." This was the advice of my oncologist, Dr. Tito Fojo, at the National Institutes of Health in Bethesda, Maryland. He fully expected the cancer to come roaring back with nothing to be done about it. Turns out, I am the sole survivor of the experimental chemotherapy protocol I began participating in just over five years ago, with fifty-six other individuals with adrenal cortical carcinoma. Until that point, I had never met anyone else with adrenal cancer and met several during my treatments. It sure is humbling and overwhelming knowing they are all now dead while I am, for some reason, alive. It gives me a great sense of awe and responsibility. Somehow, I need to feel worthy of being the lone survivor. What great thing can I do to benefit others during my remaining time on this earth?

I continue to be followed at NIH where I meet with Dr. Fojo regularly. We have become wonderful friends. In fact, he and his wife, Dr. Bates, came to our home two years ago, and Dr. Fojo spoke at a luncheon

I organized for over two hundred cancer survivors as part of the Bonita Springs Relay for Life. It was one of the proudest moments of my life. As the Survivorship Chair for the committee (Chuck was Co-Chair for the overall event committee), my story became well known and I was awarded the Annual Courage Award by the Naples Area American Cancer Society two years in a row. The recognition was great, but I sure wish I had not experienced what it took to earn it.

To rid my body of at least one reason to develop cancers and infections, I decided a few months ago to undergo breast reconstructive surgery using my own body fat to build breasts. The best in the country at this DIEP flap procedure are in San Antonio, a convenient drive from where Rick and Susan Stacy live. They insisted we stay with them during the expected three weeks of surgery and follow-up. During our stay, Chuck and I have been laughing with them over old stories and relishing every second of their company. We are so grateful to have picked up so many friendships along our journey together, and to be able to witness their lives evolve. Our lives—both ours and theirs—have changed so much in the time we've known them.

Sitting here, under an umbrella, I'm focusing on the beauty of the scene. The recently planted palm trees framing a waterfall across the pool from me provides comfort and escape for my thoughts. My body is in a state of complete exhaustion. Infection is roaring and, at the moment, in charge. Between Chuck and Susan providing near constant nursing care, with the help and advice of a wound care clinic in Marble Falls, I am on a slow path to recovery. Even with so much loving support, it's hard to not get discouraged. I'm working on developing patience.

Chuck is sitting a few feet away, clicking away on his computer.

"Do you ever think about the days when I still had real breasts? You must miss them...you were so fond of the girls," I say.

Chuck begins to smile—I love his smile—but not wanting to make me feel inadequate due to my lack of real mammaries, he stops short of a full grin. Trying to be sensitive to my situation, it's obvious he does not know what to say.

"You called them *pups*; you liked it when their noses got cold," I pester.

Chuck can't help but launch into a laugh, but is careful in his response. "I love you just the way you are, even without breasts. You did not have to put yourself through another fourteen hours of surgery for me," he says.

"I know you love me no matter what, and I so appreciate that you have always made me feel attractive even when I know I'm not. But I needed to do this surgery for me. I need to feel like a woman; to see myself as a woman when I look in the mirror. Without breasts, even fake ones, all I would see is my hideous roadmap of scars from so many surgeries that I've lost count. You say it doesn't matter to you, and I know you work hard to think that way, but I must see myself worthy of your intimate feelings for me? Breasts are important to my self-image."

"You are my velveteen rabbit," Chuck says with a warm smile. "When I look at you, I see the girl I met at a teenage drinking party all those years ago."

"Tell me the truth, do you miss holding real breasts?"

"Well, you sometimes have real breasts in my dreams, but I try not to go there."

I can't help but smile. His blue eyes and good nature always lift my spirits. I would have given up long ago if not for him.

"Remember the time when we were first dating, we were walking back to my mom's house on Robie Street in Bath, New York? Snow was falling. Flakes the size of quarters. We walked under a tree...I pulled on a branch and dumped snow all over you?" I say and relive the feeling of young love, of the exhilarating fun and a cold, snowy kiss that melted my heart.

"Yes, thank you for reminding me, I still owe you for that one. As I recall, we had just left another teenage drinking party," he points out.

"I don't remember doing much drinking at those parties, mainly socializing," I say.

"Yes, you have always been a great socializer. We rarely drank enough to get drunk."

"Life was so simple, then," I observe.

"Yes, it sure was."

Chuck's eyes wander deep into the past.

"Remember when I had my breasts removed," I say, jolting him forward in time to a much harder memory. "We were living in San Diego. People from church brought meals each day. You and the boys would stand at the front door salivating for whatever was about to be delivered. Always great food."

"I was just thinking of the time in Nashville when you nearly bled to death."

"Ha. Now there's a happy memory. I'll never forget walking out of that Cracker Barrel, looking down and noticing I was wet with blood where they had made the catheter insertion in my groin. A moment later, blood was running down my leg. I can still see the pool of blood expanding around me on the sidewalk. Then, you put me in the car when I wanted you to call 911, and drove me back to the hospital. It's a wonder I lived."

"Yes, and you pestered me so much while I was trying to drive, I got on the highway going in the wrong direction. I was driving over 100 miles an hour with my hand in your crotch trying to keep you from bleeding out. When we arrived at Vanderbilt Hospital, the inside of the Toyota Camry looked like the Bonnie and Clyde car covered with blood. The only thing missing was the bullet holes."

"You are just never willing to ask for help when you need it."

"I know, I need to get better about that."

"We have so many wonderful friends in each of the places we have lived over the years. Each place was so special. Our time in California, Iowa, Tennessee, Florida...if I had known how hard this surgery was going to be, and that I would end up with such awful infection problems, I'm not sure I would have gone through with it."

"Does no good to think like that. Focus on the idea that using your own body fat to build breasts will save you from future surgeries."

"True. My immune system has rejected three sets of breast implants over the past fifteen years. That part makes sense but I'm so prone to infection. You have become quite the expert in wound care. Hate putting you through it. I know it's hard on you—dealing with the gore."

"Don't beat yourself up about it. I don't mind. I just do what I have to do. We will get through this and you will be much happier. I just need a sexy nurse outfit to keep your attention."

We both laugh.

"I'm so sick of being attached to this wound-vacuum pump and carrying it everywhere I go."

"Well, it is helping with the healing process," Chuck offers.

"Not fast enough. We have imposed on the Stacys for so much longer than I ever expected. Surgery and follow-up was supposed to take three weeks at most. It's been three months! Rick and Susan are such great friends. I hope we don't wear out our welcome," I complain.

"I very much enjoy being with them. Some of the greatest people on the planet. Helping Rick with projects around here has kept my mind busy."

"He told me he appreciates you being here because your skills and eagerness to work have inspired him. It's amazing how much this place has changed since we arrived. It was already nice but now it is a beautiful garden paradise."

I begin pointing to various projects Chuck participated in to some extent over the past three months.

"Contractors did the bulk of this stonework around the pool area, but you helped move tons of dirt and rock to complete the lawn," I begin.

"Didn't think you had noticed. You were out of it a good part of the time."

"I noticed. You dug up and replanted several of these new trees after they were put in incorrectly and did plenty of other landscaping. You installed those fans on the portico and completed the new bathroom in the garage. Also, you and Rick worked together digging trenches to bury drain lines for the downspouts in 113-degree heat. I thought you were both crazy."

"It was a tad warmish. Luckily we had plenty of Shiner Bock beer to maintain needed bodily fluids."

"Ha, yeah, a bit warmish. Don't think beer is the proper fluid under those conditions."

"Really? You are reading the wrong health articles."

I can't help but laugh at him.

"Rick told me it would have taken him years to get around to doing all of the things on his own that you and he have accomplished in a few months."

"That makes me feel good. I love doing this sort of stuff and it is fun to spend time working with Rick. He's the funniest guy on the planet— don't tell him I said that."

We take a bit of time to soak in the scene.

"It's a good thing you placed all of our stuff in storage before leaving Florida to come here," I say.

"Well, with the house we were renting well into the foreclosure process, I figured it was the smartest thing to do. Especially since we expected to move somewhere, we just did not know where," Chuck reasons.

"We are a couple of gypsies right now without an address to call our own."

"Yeah…working our way around the country doing odd jobs. Might start playing a squeeze-box. Can you tell fortunes?" Chuck jokes. "Yes, it is a strange feeling to not quite be sure where we are going to live next. Rick wants us to buy a lot in this neighborhood and become Texans."

"So does Susan. Sure is tempting. I love it here, but we are moving to Virginia. Brian has threatened to start having kids and I want to spend every possible minute with my grandchildren. There's no telling how much time I might have. I know this cancer is going to get me at some point. Even Dr. Martin has said that. Plus, Greg and Jen have moved to Virginia. It will be so great to have all of us within close distance."

"Yes dear, we will move to Virginia. But first, I'm looking forward to spending a few months in upstate New York."

"Yes, it will be fun to be back in our old stompin' grounds," I say.

"Do you really think Dolores wants us to make use of her extra house in Appalachin?"

"She insists."

"Maybe the mafia will have another one of their big meetings there while we are in town. FBI swarming the place, that would sure add some excitement," Chuck quips.

"That famous mob meeting is the only reason anyone has ever heard of Appalachin, New York. The population might be a thousand in that town...if you count the cows."

"Hey, don't make fun, our hometowns aren't much bigger."

We laugh.

"Dolores won't accept any money. She just wants us to house-sit for her and work on our book. She calls her Appalachin house *The Love Shack*."

"Oooh, I like the sound of that," Chuck says and begins to sing the old song by the B-52s.

"You will have to be sure to work on some projects for her while we are there as a payback."

"Of course, my handyman skills are sure coming in handy this year. Makes our living the gypsy-life possible."

Our cell phone rings. Chuck holds the screen toward me so I can see our younger son, Greg, is calling. Chuck answers.

"Hey kid, what's going on?"

After a brief pause, "Oh, you are both on the line...Okay, I will put you on speaker phone. Your mom is sitting here next to me." Then, to me, "Greg and Jen say they have some news for us."

Chuck positions the phone between us and pushes the button for speakerphone. I am immediately tingling with excitement, anticipating what I hope the news might be.

"Okay, you two, spill the beans. What's going on?" I say with mock sternness.

"First of all, happy birthday, Mom," Greg says.

"Happy birthday, Debbie!" echoes Jen.

"Thank you. You are now my favorite son and daughter-in-law since I have not yet heard from Brian and Erin."

"Well, I am pretty sure this news will put us way ahead in the competition for favorite status."

"Okay, let's hear it."

"So, we just wanted to tell you...Jen is pregnant."

I scream with delight.

"This is the greatest news I have ever received!"

For a moment, it feels like my heart is simply going to burst. So much joy; joy for Greg and Jen, and joy for Chuck and I who are going to be grandparents—*grandparents*! And over top of all of that, a layer of deep gratitude. God had promised me this day, all those years ago: "*And you shall live to see your children's children.*"

God promised and here I am, alive and grandmother to an unborn child. I have made it. Made it through dozens of surgeries, chemo, and one devastating prognosis after another. If anyone had told us how much faith, grit and gumption it would take to keep me alive, I don't know if we would have signed ourselves up for it. Or maybe we would have, if they'd also told us about how close we would get as a couple, or how much fun it would be to watch our sons grow up, and fall in love with wonderful women. My heart is so full of God's grace and goodness.

"Greg, how long have you two known about this?"

"For a few weeks. Wanted to wait for your birthday."

"I never thought I would live long enough to see you and Brian graduate high school, let alone get married and have children of your own."

"Well, you were promised, Mom."

"Yes, I will never forget the day I put my finger down on that verse in the Bible. It was the worst day in my life, and my best, until now. This is the best news ever!"

We hang up with them and look at each other in awe.

"I can't believe it."

"Neither can I."

Returning to the moment, I look at the scenery about us with a whole new perspective...with renewed hope for the future. I'm a grandmother to a child due in January.

"Remember when you and Cathy Williams were stalking Brian and Erin while Brian was proposing?" Chuck asks.

He is back on the nostalgia tour.

"Yes, that was so much fun, hiding behind telephone poles and cars while Brian was proposing in front of the bar where they first met."

"I'm so thankful Brian shared that with us."

"Yes," I say. "We have two very special sons. I am so happy right now I could burst."

"It never ceases to amaze me how different Brian and Greg are from one another, both wonderful in their own way. They each married their perfect match," Chuck says.

"That's for sure. Their weddings were fun, but way too stressful. It is much more enjoyable to attend other people's weddings. It's great to have no real responsibilities for the festivities. I should always be thankful I had the chance to see them take place," I say, trying to regain proper perspective.

"So many times, I have questioned whether it is worth going through all of the suffering to stay alive but today's news has renewed my will to stay alive. I am going to be a grandmother. You are going to be a grandfather...Mimi, I want to be called Mimi. What do you want to be called by our grands?"

"I don't know. What's wrong with just being called *Grandpa*?"

"No, it has to be something special. How about *Papa*?"

"Maybe...wasn't that Hemingway's nickname?"

"Yes."

"Perfect."

We laugh.

"It's going to be a girl," Chuck says.

"Huh? What makes you say that?" I ask.

"Remember yesterday when we were at the dance recital for Madeline? Rick and Susan were beaming with pride for their granddaughter...well, it occurred to me...watching all those little girls bouncing around the stage in Pepto-Bismal pink that I would love to have a little girl. I grew up with all brothers and we had two sons. I have never had the little girl experience. Somehow, I just know it will be a girl and she will love the color pink."

Chuck sure is convincing. Having a granddaughter would be a dream come true. I wouldn't trade my sons for anything but I so wanted a little girl of my own.

"Someday, I want take our grandchildren to Disney World...if I live long enough."

"We will, I'm sure," Chuck says, then pointing past the pool to the field beyond, "Debbie, look!"

Three small deer step out of the dense grove of cedar and thorn into the open and begin to graze on Rick's well-watered grass. My heart swells at their beauty. They are an omen of wonderful things to come.

The call came this morning. Jen's water broke. Our first grandchild, a girl just as Chuck predicted, has already been named Addison and is arriving over three weeks early.

Greg and Jen are in the process of moving from a small apartment to a house, which has been extra difficult because the doctors told Jen she needs to be on bedrest. All their belongings are in their new residence, but much remains to be done. After her water broke this morning, Jen called to tell me her midwife said to go to the hospital. Of course, being a Thursday, both Greg and Chuck are at work. Jen's sister—we call her Georgie—picked me up and the three of us drove to the hospital.

Since Addison is arriving nearly a month early, there are a good number of necessary baby items yet to be purchased for the nursery. Greg will pick up bedding and a few more essentials before meeting us at the hospital.

It's funny—after so many surgeries, I hate hospitals. I hate the sterile gray walls, the clipboards and stiff uniforms; the sound of machines whirring and beeping, but most of all I hate the *smell*. The smell of a hospital reminds me of uncertainty, doubt and of the prevailing possibility of unwelcome endings.

But today is different. Today, those neutral walls look brighter to me, like a clean slate ready to write a new and hopeful story on. In fact, the hallway walls in this maternity ward are covered with actual baby footprints. Footprints of babies born here over the years. Addison's footprints will soon be added to the gallery. So, today is different, the familiar nausea-inducing hospital scent now feels like fresh-washed linens in a just-made bed; the perfect safe place to welcome a fragile newborn. This hospital room was specially constructed for new beginnings, and staffed with a welcoming committee in scrubs—today, it's just for us, just for my soon to be born granddaughter.

And the real bonus, for once, instead of being the patient, I am going to be one of the ones in the waiting room, sitting on pins and needles— excited pins and needles, of course.

For several weeks, I have been knitting a blanket for sweet baby Addison's arrival, but due to her ahead-of-schedule entry into the wide world, I have not yet finished it. Although I have purchased an abundance of grandbaby items—after all, having raised boys, it's hard to say no to both the color pink *and* a good deal— I also want my grandchildren to have things I've stitched together for them with my own two hands. To add to all the excitement, Erin recently told us she is also pregnant; due in July. There are two grandbabies to prepare for! God is raining blessings on me. Life is so good.

Greg doesn't think he can handle being in the delivery room for the actual birth, so when it's time to push I'll join Georgie as the other half of Jen's support team. Georgie had a baby three months ago (a sweet baby boy named Isaiah), so between the two of us we should be quite the "super-delivery duo!" Jen's epidural only worked on half of her body, which means she must take pain medications to account for the rest of the pain—it's leaving her pretty loopy. The doctor may attempt a second epidural later, but that will depend on time.

We've been taking turns filtering in and out of the delivery room, checking on Jen and her progress. She has been in labor for nearly twenty-four hours, which reminds me of my first delivery.

Last night they administered a second epidural, which provided Jen with some relief, and made it possible for her to get some rest while she waited. Poor Georgie, who was up all night as mothers of a newborn often are anyway, is curled up on the delivery room floor catching some much-needed shut eye. Such a good sister—reminds me of my own.

"I feel like I need to push," Jen says.

We're about to meet our precious bundle of joy: my first granddaughter.

"Time for you boys to clear out," I say.

Chuck says a quick goodbye to Jen. Greg leans in for a kiss and one last round of encouragement. As they leave the room, I scurry over to the corner and wake Georgie. Helping her up, I aim her toward her battle-station across from mine at the head of Jen's bed.

After exhaustive pushing, Addison still has not arrived.

"Jen," the doctor says, "I want you to give one more good push. But if she doesn't come out this time, we may need to go in and get her or I might have to perform an episiotomy. That basically means I'll have to make a surgical cut to widen the opening for the baby to pass through."

Jen nods bravely, as Georgie and I continue to cheerlead.

"I know you're tired, but you're almost done."

"So close."

"She'll be here before you know it, and then this will all be worth it."

Somewhere over our soothing murmurs, my ears began to pick up the more business-like hum of hospital staff conversation.

"Mom's blood pressure is still too high. Doesn't seem to be coming down."

"Mom's blood pressure? Look at the baby's. Doc, I think you should come look at this."

Then the hum stops. My heart quickens and begins to pound against my chest. Silence in a hospital room is still one of the things that makes me nervous. I glance back over my shoulder to peek at the face of the doctor, intently studying the numbers. He looks calm. Turning back around, I catch Georgie's eyes above the hospital bed; we exchange fleeting, worried glances. Still stroking Jen's hand, I notice the door is opening with more frequency. We're in serious trouble here. Dear God, be with us, I pray.

Looking around the room, I realize our entourage is growing to quite a crowd. More and more nurses come in, go out of the room and return with others. Tension is building. It's almost suffocating. I feel them all willing, praying my granddaughter to be born alive. The doctor's voice jostles me back.

"Jen, I'm going to need to perform the episiotomy. We also need to get a better read on your baby's heartbeat, so we're going to use a fetal heart monitor that will screw into her head. I know it sounds scary, but it's very safe and much more accurate than the belly monitor we're using now."

A swarm of nurses join the doctor at the foot of the bed. Georgie and I lean in and whisper calmly to Jen. The doctor performs the procedure quickly. I re-experience my own episiotomy from when Brian was born.

"Okay, Jen, it's time to push one more time. We need to get this baby out. It's important that it happen now."

Glancing around the room, I am amazed at the bevy of delivery staff at the ready: scanning faces, looking at the monitors, I search for flickers of information. Things are not going well, not well at all, that much I know. But something is also telling me everything will be okay. There is a part of me at complete peace in the center of the storm. I direct my attention back to Jen.

"It's almost over Jen. You can do this," I say with confidence. "Let's meet our little girl."

Jen takes a deep breath, squeezes our hands with herculean strength, pushes her elbows back with sheer primal determination reverberating across her face. She's doing it!

"That's it! That's it. She's out." I hear the doctor say.

I am at once flooded with both relief and profound joy. The moment is here. A moment I've been told by so many doctors and others I would never live to see. Abrupt commotion immediately shocked me back into reality.

"The cord is wrapped around her neck. Nurse! Get over here."

The room disintegrates into a type of well-ordered chaos. The doctor and two nurses lean intently over the baby, while more swoop in around Jen with post-delivery necessities, and still more join us at the head of the bed, reaching for monitors and moving machines.

Georgie and I watch as the staff scoops up Addison and moves her to the warmer. Why isn't she crying yet? I step closer to see what is going on, and am startled to see she is not moving and the palest shade of blue I've ever seen. Before I can react, I am intercepted by a very determined nurse who commands me back to my place with Jen. Georgie and I stare at each other for a terrified moment, knowing that, once again, silence in a hospital room isn't a good thing. Addison isn't breathing. Seconds tick by like entire minutes.

"What's going on? What's happening?" Jen asks.

"Everything will be fine," I assure her.

Georgie and I do our best to soothe and distract her as we wait for something to report. Anything to report.

"Dear God," I close my eyes and whisper. "Be with her as you've been with me."

And with that prayer out, the room is filled with the ear-piercing siren song only a baby girl can produce. As Georgie, Jen, and I dissolve into joyful, relieved tears, the flurry of nurses continues working around us. We are beyond terrified, ecstatic, and are just so ready to finally hold her.

"Well," I joke with Jen. "It's a good thing I've almost finished kitting that blanket."

Thank God the birth of Aubrey, seven months later on the fourth of July, is much less traumatic. She arrives so soon after Erin's arrival at the hospital, Chuck and I are barely there in time. I do not get to witness this birth, but do hear Aubrey's first cry.

Two and a half years later, my youngest granddaughter, Layla, is born in the same hospital as her sister, Aubrey, and cousin, Addison. The footprints of my three little deer are on the walls of the maternity ward at Bon Secours DePaul Medical Center in Norfolk, Virginia.

# CHAPTER 10

# MR. WHIPPLE

### *(Debbie)*

I t's November 2010, and Chuck and I are comfortably settled into our home in Chesapeake, Virginia Beach, loving life as grandparents. We are also preparing to meet with another team of doctors in Bethesda, Maryland. Last month I traveled there to the National Institutes of Health for routine chest and abdominal CT scans. I go three to four times a year for follow-up visits now, after participating in a clinical trial there. Although the doctors there take exceptional care of me, it's always a time fraught with anxiety; thankfully, I normally end up leaving with an "everything is stable" report.

This time, however, something unusual was detected in my liver. My doctor didn't seem overly concerned, and persuaded me not to obsess about it. We planned to look more closely at the area via MRI.

Meanwhile, I was also due for a colonoscopy. (Recommended every three years for me. Aren't I lucky?) I found a gastroenterologist here in Virginia Beach and met with him to get it scheduled. He offered to do an endoscopy while I was "under." Initially, I declined, reasoning it was probably unnecessary since I'm so carefully monitored at NIH. For some reason, I changed my mind—which I've learned at this point to attribute, without question, to divine intervention—and notified the doctor to add the endoscopy to his schedule.

I fully expected to receive a report stating a polyp or two had been removed from my colon, but never anticipated anything sinister would be discovered. Thankfully, the doctor was aware of my extensive cancer history, and decided to biopsy a few areas that caught his attention, just to make sure he didn't overlook anything. He said he was surprised when the pathology report described malignant cells on the "Ampulla of Vater." I chuckled to myself, thinking of the sinister character from Star Wars with the soundalike name. Instead of a helmeted bad guy dressed in black, I'm informed this is the area where the pancreatic duct and common bile duct merge to empty into the small intestine. I would much rather have heard an explanation of why Darth wore a cape.

Feeling fine, with no symptoms, I was shocked by the news. A subsequent endoscopic ultrasound was performed, and the results were encouraging. The lymph nodes sampled were benign, and the small tumor doesn't appear to have invaded the pancreas. I've been informed the only option is to go after this surgically; there is no question I will have the surgery at NIH where I've been so well taken care of in the past.

Unfortunately, the MRI has returned and didn't bring good news either. There is another tumor in my liver. After my case was presented to the surgical tumor board, it was determined the best approach would be a modified "Whipple", and a wedge resection of my liver; both to be done in the same surgery. I will have the surgery on the 23rd of November.

Of course, because real life doesn't stop at the sound of a "whipple", I am scrambling to get things done before we leave for Bethesda. I'm doing all the things I may not feel up to doing after my surgery. Chuck and I plan to drive to Bethesda Sunday evening, and stay in a hotel since I must be at the hospital before 7:00 a.m. My sister is driving down from Pennsylvania to spend the weekend with me, and will follow us to NIH to be there for my surgery. My father and stepmother will meet us at the hospital Monday.

While I admit I'm dreading the surgery, and would love to slow down the clock, I can't wait to see my sister. I'm sure she will keep me very distracted. She is one of my biggest cheerleaders.

A full battery of tests turned up more unexpected news—and delayed my surgery multiple times. It appeared there are some additional tumors that needed attention. Tissue was harvested from one tumor in my liver, one in my central chest, and one located between my heart and the chest wall. The procedure to access the tumor in my central chest was especially difficult. My breathing was controlled by an endotracheal tube so the doctor performing the biopsy could more safely insert the needle between my heart and diaphragm. The insertion had to be perfectly timed to take place between beats of my heart—oh, the drama!

Thankfully, the biopsy from my test was reviewed by the surgical team and determined to be noncancerous. Thank God! The plan now is to do a liver resection and Whipple surgery tomorrow, the fourteenth of December. I have met with a cardiologist, the pulmonary team, taken special supplements and done everything else required to prepare me for the operation.

We asked our friends and family to pray God will guide the hands of my doctors, Dr. Russell Langan and Dr. Itzhak Avital. The surgeon told me the liver resection will be very difficult (I asked him if he meant for *him* or for *me*...and he replied, "for both of us"). He explained the surgery will be challenging since the tumor is resting against the portal vein. He is concerned as to whether he will be able to remove all the tumor because of its proximity to the vein. I'm relying on God to see us all through this, but I would be lying if I said I wasn't scared.

Anyway, now that I have met with the surgeons, the cardiologist and various nurses, I will be checking out of the hospital for the evening. I've been given another pass to return first thing tomorrow morning. The head surgeon gave me permission to have one glass of wine with dinner tonight (he did *not*, however, specify the size of the glass!).

I'm a little sad to think I may be in the hospital for Christmas, but if it ensures I will be around for future Christmases, it's a sacrifice I'm willing to make. Little Addison's first birthday was this past Saturday, and I was so happy my surgery had been delayed so I could be home for that. I may be biased, but I firmly believe my granddaughters are the sweetest little girls in the world. I am bound and determined to get every Christmas with them that I can.

### *(Chuck)*

It has been a long day already. The head surgeon came out a little while ago to give me an update. He began by saying "everything is fine." He then went on to say that only now (after five-plus hours of surgery) have they succeeded in the opening of the abdomen. This part of the process should have taken less than two hours.

This surgeon is one of the best in the world. He is used to challenging cases, and usually discounts the difficulty of procedures, but the amazed expression on his face added emphasis when he said, "This has been a very, very difficult surgery, so far."

He explained the challenges are a result of a few things. First, the prevalence of adhesions and scar tissue throughout her abdomen (due to her numerous previous surgeries). Second, her liver is unlike any other, having regenerated with unique proportions and orientation after ninety percent of it was removed. This adds a puzzle they must solve before the tumor there can be removed.

To my great relief, he said he believes both the adrenal metastatic tumor in the liver, and the ampulla carcinoma of the pancreas (in the common bile duct), will be successfully removed.

Finally, he stated this is all good news, but there are seven to nine hours of surgery remaining.

Despite the stress, I feel great strength from the notes of support from so many friends and family. This morning, I was with Debbie in pre-op. I was struck by her bravery as she maintained mental focus on her medical situation despite being so frightened. We are both floating on the many thoughts and prayers of the vast circle of friends and family we're so lucky to have.

Three days removed, I am equal parts exhausted and grateful. It has been a great day—especially considering the third day out from surgery is usually the toughest. Debbie spent most of the day sitting in a recliner, but is feeling triumphant because she also walked three times. The medical team is impressed with her progress.

The more I hear from the doctors and nurses here, the more I realize the extent to which we had taken for granted that this surgery would simply take place, the cancer would be removed, and life would go on. It turns out, this was "the largest scale operation undertaken by this surgical team in the past six months." In fact, only twenty-five people have undergone both a liver resection and a Whipple procedure during one operation (in this country) in the past twenty-five years.

Medical types show up at her room, and the conversation begins with, "I just read her surgical report, and I can't believe how well she looks." Then her extensive medical history (the fact she has survived eight primary cancers, and nine metastatic cancer episodes including several major surgeries) adds to their astonishment. Thank you, God!

I also realized how grateful I am for Debbie's father and stepmother, Don and Harriet Pruden, for all they have done to support me, and for being there for Debbie during this challenging time. Since Debbie's battle with cancer began more than two decades ago, they have routinely dropped everything to travel to wherever we happened to be living to help. Whenever the situation has been dire, they have been there. We love them for that.

As far as this surgery went, the doctors have brought us the best news. The pathology is back on the tumors that were removed, and we couldn't have asked for a better result. The large liver tumor was totally resected with all clean margins; in other words, they were able to remove all the cancer. The ampullary cancer ended up being a "stage one"...a small tumor. Thirteen sampled lymph nodes were clear, and the bile ducts were not affected adversely.

Debbie's oncologist stopped by to see us a few minutes ago. He promises 2011 will be cancer-free. He is, however, concerned about 2012. He expects that adrenal cancer will likely come roaring back in 2012. Obviously, it's time to regain perspective. I question, how are we to rise to the gift of a year or so of relative good health? We have done this so many times over the past twenty-four years; living wonderful bits of semi-normalcy between cancer episodes. How do we make the most of the blessing this time?

### (Debbie)

My doctor told me to make plans for the summer. He promised I would feel better, and that 2011 will be a good year for me. I'm so glad I believed him. We've had a full schedule since spring; one that will continue for the rest of the year—which will culminate in a trip with my sister to the Amalfi Coast of Italy at the end of September. Our dear friends from Texas, Susan and Rick Stacy, visited us the end of April and we had a great time with them. Shortly thereafter, we took a beach vacation to the Outer Banks with my sister, her husband, and three other crazy, fun-loving couples. My friend Roxanne always says, "laughter is the best medicine." If so, I should be cured completely after my week with those nuts! I had anticipated a lot of silliness, and laughter. I was not let down.

Spring spilled over into summer. Chuck and I rejoiced at a family wedding in May; we toasted with champagne at an Iowa wedding in the heat of July. We got home just in time to celebrate little Aubrey's first birthday (our second granddaughter). Addison, now nineteen months old, is growing and changing so fast. It's been delightful watching both granddaughters grow and develop their own unique personalities. They interact well with each other, and I hope and pray they remain close friends as I was with my cousins over the years.

And my sister—there's no one like my sister. Chuck and I drove to her house (west of Philly) after the last time we left NIH, planning to spend the weekend. Nancy knows just what to do to make me feel better; she can always make me laugh! We stayed a whole extra day and spent it shopping. At least the malls were cool inside. Chuck and Chris went golfing (crazy...far too hot).

So, we've just returned from two days at NIH undergoing a PET scan, CT scan, blood tests, and clinic appointments with my oncologist and surgeon. The news wasn't what I had hoped for, but we have a plan. Oh, how I do love a plan!

There is a small, grape-sized (what is it with the fruit?) tumor in my liver. I will be admitted in a couple of weeks for a work up, then will undergo a liver ablation. This procedure involves inserting a probe into the liver to *burn* the tumor using radio waves...believe it or not, that's much less invasive than what I've had done in the past. I have undergone RFA (radio-frequency ablation) twice before, so I'm somewhat prepared for what lies ahead. I'll remain in the hospital a couple days to be monitored, then will hopefully be on my way.

For now, the nurse brought me a new keyboard and mouse; I select the right mode on the TV, and I have instant internet access...not bad! I've been catching up on email, and checking out all the happenings of my friends and family on Facebook. I also brought my knitting; I signed up for a knitting class back in Virginia Beach, and have been working on a project I've ripped out *countless* times. Think I have finally figured out the pattern—hope I don't get too loopy from pain medication, and goof it all up!

We're finally back home in Chesapeake. I probably should have stayed in the hospital over the weekend as I've been running a fever since I got home, but Chuck needed to get back for work—his company has been understanding and flexible. That's been a blessing. Truth be told, I don't think I could have stood one more night in the hospital. I am so tired of being poked and prodded. I'm so looking forward to the comfort of my own bed.

My doctor left on vacation Monday, and has called several times to check on me and to reassure me that what I am experiencing is normal. He says my shoulder pain is not a bad thing; it means they burned part of the diaphragm—part of getting a *good burn* of the tumor in my liver. Feel the burn. (Is it bad I still prefer to get that through a workout at the gym?)

Erin and Jen brought dinner Saturday evening. That was much appreciated, since I had little in the house to eat. Even if I could find something, I wasn't up to cooking. Though I felt well enough to make spaghetti sauce this morning, things began to go downhill after that. Erin's parents smoked a turkey today, because they had the whole Williams clan in for Sunday dinner. They sent Brian over with hearty portions of food from their meal—a very thoughtful and caring family. We are blessed to have such a great support system.

Speaking of which, Chuck reminded me that next week is our thirty-fourth wedding anniversary. What a blessing he has been. I don't know how I would weather the storms without his unwavering love and support. I wonder if he had any idea all those years ago what he was in for. Thank God, he's a man of integrity and commitment. I am truly blessed.

# CHAPTER 11

# LIFE, LOSS, AND CHEMO

### *(Debbie)*

This is one of the hardest things I've ever had to write. On the first of November, I lost my father: one of my strongest supporters, encouragers, and cheerleaders. I can't even begin to express the overwhelming grief and loss I feel, especially during a time when I have so many challenges with my health

The doctors have found fluid in my lungs, and suspect I may have an abscess in my liver. The liver probing didn't reveal an infection, but cultures from the samples taken indicate an organism is growing. I went back on heavy duty antibiotics for two weeks, and had a follow-up scan. The antibiotics make me so sick. I not only have stomach and digestive issues, but also mouth sores, difficulty eating, drinking, and extreme fatigue. I was so glad to be done with them. Then, the very same day, I received the call my father had died unexpectedly at home. It was such a shock because he was in good physical shape—exercised religiously, took great care of himself, and stayed on top of his health.

Naturally, I just wanted to get home to New York to be with my family. I was about to cancel my scans and deal with my health later, when I began to think about how my father was always adamant about me taking care of myself. I reluctantly made the stop at NIH to undergo the scheduled scans. Apparently, there is still something going on in

118

my liver; no sign of tumors, just some reactive process to the ablation I underwent a few months ago. Knowing I had to get to New York, my doctor wrote me another prescription for more antibiotics, and told me to come back afterward for another attempt at inserting a drain into my liver.

We traveled from Bethesda to my brother's house, near Hershey, Pennsylvania, and then on up to New York the following day to plan a funeral. It has been a difficult time, and I'm struggling with such an overwhelming sense of sadness and loss. My father and stepmother have been with me through all the years of my cancer struggles, often dropping everything to sit at my bedside through various surgeries and procedures. Knowing I won't see his smiling face and hear his words of encouragement, especially during future stays at NIH, makes it even harder to go back and continue the fight—but I know Dad would want me to do everything I can to maintain a good, healthy, quality of life.

My positive outlook is not bulletproof. There have been days when I've questioned whether all of this is worth it. I'm embarrassed to admit this, but a few weeks ago I found myself questioning the very existence of a loving God. In my conversation yesterday with my oncologist, I stated that I have always been a fighter, and I've never been this ready to give up. He laughed, and reminded me of the various times while undergoing chemotherapy in 2004 that I was ready to stop the treatments, as I could not see the light at the end of the tunnel. The reality is it was only because of everyone's unyielding love, and forceful encouragement, that I continued with that program. It has bought me five years, so far. There were bumps along the way, but I felt relatively well, and enjoyed my life during those years. I do not possess an indestructible, positive outlook. I don't believe anyone truly does, and don't understand how anyone could survive such health challenges without a community of faith, and network of support.

I am always reluctant to share this reality, as I hear from so many people looking to me as an example. However, if I don't share the essential truths of what it takes to survive, I'm not doing anyone any favors.

At this point, though, I still can't help but reflect on the countless blessings God has given me over these many years through various doctors, backed up by the unswerving love and support of family and friends. I'm thankful and know God loves me, and has already forgiven me for my weakness and moments of doubt.

It's Sunday afternoon. Doctors at the National Institutes of Health have installed two drains in my liver to remove the large pockets of fluid. I may have to remain in the hospital until the middle of next week, which is not the most irritating news. There is a chance Chuck might have to learn how to administer the antibiotics at home by IV, and he really doesn't want to add that to his nursing resume.

Chuck left for home a couple of hours ago. I had quite a pity party yesterday when it was clear I was not going home, and that he had to go home without me to finish up a project at work. Dr. Fojo stopped in last night to bring us up to date on the results from the latest CT scan, and talk about what is planned next. He said the small amount of fluid that has drained so far does not look like an abscess. However, he said there is a third collection of fluid in the liver that may also have to be drained, which would mean another trip to Special Procedures to have yet another drain inserted into my liver. All will depend on the results of another CT scheduled for Monday morning. News of facing another procedure combined with the realization I will be on my own here for a few days has started me down the "woe-is-me" path. I spent the evening feeling sorry for myself.

This morning, I decided I need to look at my situation from a different point of view. My wallowing in self-pity is not only making things harder for me, but is making it extremely difficult for Chuck. So, I'm counting my blessings...and there are many.

Instead of railing against God for allowing the struggles in my life, I'm praising him. I have so much to be thankful for: this wonderful medical facility with state-of-the-art technology and research, for one, and my outstanding medical team and the excellent care I receive. If I need a medical test, it is scheduled in a timely manner, and the results are available quickly. I am not denied any medication or diagnostic test because of insurance constraints. My husband has been at my side through over twenty years of dealing with cancer issues. He constantly reminds me how much he loves me, and I have loving and supportive family and friends. Yes, this past year has been challenging, but I am feeling hopeful again. I just need to get over this bump in the road.

Amazingly, when I changed my attitude, things began to look up. Doctors from my clinical team and the infectious disease team stopped in, and confirmed there does not seem to be any abscess. There is no evidence so far of any bacteria growing from the cultures being observed in the lab. I should be able to leave on Tuesday. All in all, they were very positive, and seemed pleased with my progress.

So, while I know it will be a long couple of days, I'm feeling more confident we're heading in the right direction, and am looking forward to going home.

It will be wonderful to sleep in my own bed; no drains, no IVs, no nurses waking me every couple of hours to start infusions or take vital signs. I get wonderful care at NIH, and the nursing staff is great, but there is no rest in a hospital. I can't wait to sit in my flannel PJs, and oversized bathrobe, and sip a cup of coffee.

I learned something quite valuable this past year. It's easy to be faithful, and trust in God's plan when you are high on the mountain, but when you sink into those valleys, and he feels so far away, despair can take over. Those are the times we need to focus on—and yes, even praise God for—our blessings and trials. He has a plan for me, and this past year of suffering is all part of it. When I couldn't find the will or energy to go to him for help, my friends and family did it for me, and kept me floating on their prayers and words of support.

### *A Tale of Two Christmases: With Great Expectations for 2012 Wilson Family Christmas letter (Chuck)*

"Chuck, it has been several years since we sent out a Christmas letter. I want you to write it—since I do everything else around here—and it had better *not* be a downer. It's already January, so call it a New Year's letter. Keep it short!" Debbie dismissed me with a backhanded wave, as if shooing a fly from a picnic plate of beans and barbecue.

"Yes, my queen," I replied, bowing my way out of the royal bedchamber.

My mind wrestled with the challenges of my assignment. "How am I going to pull this off? How am I ever going to convince people that a year resembling gothic portrayals of hell was actually a good one?"

After all, 2011 was:

- A year of recovery anchored to a thirteen-hour operation that occurred just prior to Christmas of 2010. The procedure combined two major surgeries (the doctors involved said it was the most difficult they had ever undertaken). Debbie spent that entire holiday season hospitalized at NIH.
- A year of dealing with the side effects of surgery and medications, wound care, infections, and a recurrence of adrenal cancer (in the liver) in July that required a radio frequency ablation (RFA) to destroy the tumor.
- Ongoing internal infection that has kept the doctors scratching their five-hundred-pound brains, and adjusting antibiotics since the RFA.

- A year in which Debbie's father, Don Pruden, passed away suddenly, and unexpectedly (in November). He and his wife, Harriet, had been a constant source of support throughout our battle with cancer—instantly traveling to wherever in the country we happened to be living.
- A year in which my brother, Harry, has continued to fight pancreatic cancer.
- A year that caused Debbie to lose hope; to question her faith.

Well, the truth is, despite everything, we did have a blessed year, but how can this be true? How can such an outlook be anything but a false front: a bright, yellow happy face painted over dark realities; lipstick smeared on a pig; the sappy verses of a silly "counting-my-blessings" Christmas song?

Well, a moment of clarity occurred in April during an exchange with Debbie's oncologist, Dr. Tito Fojo.

"This whole recovery experience has been so awful—I wish I had never had the surgery. I completely missed Christmas with my family; my life has been turned upside-down. I can't eat..." Debbie related to Tito.

Tito responded, "If you had not had that surgery, we would not be having this conversation because you would not be alive."

I think that conversation is why we went to such great lengths to make this Christmas extra special. Debbie made every special recipe she could recall of her mother's, and our grandmothers' fudge, cookies, pies, and casseroles. We even bought a live tree, and thoroughly decorated the house, inside and out.

From another perspective, 2011 was:

- A year when our granddaughters, Addison and Aubrey, were a constant source of purpose and great joy for both of us.
- A year when many of you followed our experience on Caring Bridge (a website specially designed for people undergoing major health challenges). It makes it possible for everyone interested

to stay informed without constant phone calls, and provide supportive notes. We can't thank everyone enough for the encouragement and love that came to us through your postings.

- A year in which Debbie felt well enough in May for us to spend a week at a beautiful beach house on the outer banks of North Carolina with four other fun couples (including sister, Nancy, and cousin, Patty).
- A year in which we attended my sister Noel's wedding in upstate New York, and the wedding of the son of our close friends (the Burmeisters) in Iowa.
- A year in which, believe it or not, Debbie endured a seventeen-mile bike ride through The Great Dismal Swamp in early July. It was much nicer than the name implies.
- A year when, despite an internal infection, Debbie traveled to Italy in September with her sister Nancy (and a supply of antibiotics).
- A year when our sons, Brian and Greg, their wives, Erin and Jennifer, and of course our beautiful granddaughters, all now own their nearby homes. We enjoy being close, and involved in their lives—we hope they do as well.
- We love our new home—especially since our gypsy days of moving every few years are officially behind us. We intend to live here until they roll us out, drooling.
- The Navy contractor I work for (can't tell you what I do because then I'd have to kill you) was extremely supportive and flexible, allowing me to work from home or make up lost time when my nursing duties for Debbie took priority.

A year ago, a perfect storm of tough times caused the flames of hope and faith to flicker. Debbie was ashamed to admit that doubts about God had crept into her thoughts—especially after all he has done for us. Thankfully, her stubborn habit of perseverance, supported by the love and encouragement of others, propelled her long enough for a season of good times to return—ablaze with life's promises—the reward for facing impossible odds with character.

Looking back from this side of 2011, it's with a sense of accomplishment. Yes, Christmas 2010 was, without a doubt, the toughest of our lives, but without it the greatness of Christmas 2011 could not have been realized

In 2012, we are looking forward to our thirty-fifth anniversary, and celebrating our vows at Keuka Chapel (where we originally married) in upstate New York. We are praying for a year of good health, and visits from friends at our Virginia home.

"When the dickens are you going to finish that letter?" I just heard from the other room.

"I'm finished, your majesty."

God bless us, every one.

## *(Debbie)*

Here we are again: 2012 has brought us more surprises. My last scans found another liver tumor, seven centimeters by seven centimeters, which is about the size of a small orange.

Unfortunately, it's growing fast, and the only thing left is the chemotherapy route. I am getting the infusions locally. Dr. Fojo recommended chemo once a week, in lower doses, to mitigate the side effects. He believes this approach will afford me a greater dose over a longer period.

Everything went well with my first chemo visit today. My daughter-in-law Jennifer dropped me off in the morning, and Chuck picked me up in the afternoon. I took along a knitting project (which killed a lot of time since I forgot the pattern, and ended up tearing out a complicated section, and reworking it until I got it right), a book, and my iPhone. Great distractions while I was being infused.

Volunteers brought lunch and snacks while I was there; it really is such a friendly place. It's a new office, with comfortable leather recliners—sunny and welcoming. The nurses in the infusion area are very nice and upbeat. They never complain, and they are constantly running and accommodating—they also have *great* senses of humor. Most of the patients are friendly, supportive, and hopeful.

Chuck and I are continuing to make plans and look to the future. We are planning to do a lot of work around the house this spring: working with a landscaper to install a patio and hot tub (a good stress reducer for Chuck). We are also having geothermal heat and air conditioning installed.

I may not lose all my hair, but it will probably thin out over the weeks. Oh well, small price to pay if this stuff works. I've been given some good nausea medication to take at home when I need it over the next six weeks, then it's back to NIH for more scans to see if it's working. If not—well, not going to visit worst case scenarios yet. I prefer to be like Scarlett O'Hara, and "think about that tomorrow!" Counting my blessings, and feeling grateful for each day.

Well, I'm three weeks into chemo, and it's beginning to kick in. I almost begged off my "4-Ever 40" group dinner this evening, which would have been a *huge* loss! My friends are a fun collection of ladies who get together once a month at one of our homes for a meal and too many laughs to count. Dinner was delicious, but I probably should have skipped the gravy.

Today was a good day at treatment (let's be honest, one of the best parts is that I still have hair). I've been thinking about my dear friend, Hank Hochstetler, in Bonita Springs, Florida. Hank never, ever complained during the times he underwent chemo. He always wore a smile, and when asked how things were going, he replied, "peachy keen."

Pretty sure Hank will forgive me if I steal his line. From now on, when someone asks how I'm doing, my answer will be, "peachy keen!"

I also finally got to meet a new friend, whom I have talked to but never met face-to-face. A fellow cancer survivor, she was asked by our pastor to reach out to me during this latest journey. We have chatted on the phone quite a few times, but keep missing each other at church. She is delightful. We quickly learned we have similar senses of humor, and could get into some trouble together. Yay—a partner in crime! Amazing how people come into your life at just the right time.

My friend Donna Murphy also popped in and spent a couple hours entertaining me. Donna has been a good friend since we were stationed here in Norfolk over thirty years ago. She was my Lamaze coach when I was pregnant with Greg, and, of course, Chuck was deployed. Donna was with me through the entire process, including the birth. She's a nurse, though she claims to "know nothin' 'bout birthin' no babies!" (Yes, another *Gone with The Wind* reference.)

Pam Mellinger, one of my "4-Ever-40" friends, called me over the weekend and offered to take me to the yarn shop, and help with a pair of socks. It all started as part of a class *she* talked me into—I call them the most expensive pair of socks I *never* made! We spent all of last Saturday afternoon knitting so, as you can tell, I'm very well taken care of here. Again, how do people face challenges without the support of family, friends, church, and even strangers? I'm blessed, that's all I can say.

While trying to knit during chemo, my multi-tasking sister keeps me busy playing Words with Friends, a scrabble game we play over the phone. I receive regular texts from Roxanne, and video texts from Jennifer and Addison. One day a week getting chemo is not enough to accomplish my knitting project with all the interruptions. I am not complaining—I feel loved and cared for.

Our landscaping project is in the works, and the spa is ordered. The electrician comes tomorrow to do the wiring for the hot tub. Now, if it ever stops raining, we will get our yard smoothed out, and reseeded.

Leaves and flowers are popping. The iris bulbs my cousin Lorraine and her husband Gerhard sent me from New York are breaking through everywhere. I'm starting to realize I didn't do a great job planning where I placed them! Oh well, at least I got them in the ground. Shocked by how many are coming up; they didn't look very alive when I opened the box.

For many years, I have been planning to repair an old children's rocker that we've been hauling around the country. Refurbished, I want to see my grandchildren use it. Chuck works with someone who is going to remake the wooden rocker part, and I found some pretty upholstery fabric on sale. A local upholstery shop has agreed to apply the fabric once I paint the wooden rocker parts. So, I stopped at Lowe's, and bought a small can of paint to match the fabric. While at Lowe's, I picked up two pots of Gerber daisies to take to chemo; one for the front desk, and one for the infusion room. Flowers always lift one's spirit, and mine are soaring today. I want to share the joy.

I met a new friend today, and we compared notes. She's a sweet, young mother who is dealing, like me, with a genetic mutation that causes tumor growth. We shared our thoughts, our faith, and a few laughs. We were so busy chatting that when my chemo finished and the nurse came to disconnect me, I told her to give me a few minutes. I ended up staying for another twenty minutes. Getting up to leave, I forgot I was tethered. The nurses got quite a charge out of the fact I didn't bolt out of the place after my treatment was over. I told them it's one of my favorite places to come now.

On my way out, I saw my doctor and the physician's assistant who insists I should be losing my hair by now. They smiled, and gave me a thumbs-up when I flipped my locks at them.

I made new curtain valances over the weekend. Well, I completed one, and it's hanging; almost finished with the others. Monday, I went fabric shopping with a friend, and purchased some material to make summer dresses for the little girls. I probably won't get started on those until this weekend since Thursdays and Fridays are always a wash-out with chemo side effects.

Chuck bought more rhubarb tonight so I guess I'll be making a pie in the morning. He loves rhubarb pie, so if I can get my hands on fresh rhubarb, I make it for him. I made one for him last week, and he said it's the best he ever had (don't tell his grandmother—it's her recipe!).

Chemotherapy has unfortunately become a way of life around here. My six treatments turned into eight, then ten, and today I completed my fourteenth session. The doctors have decided it's the last treatment for now. The side effects are too awful, and we're not sure what is to be gained by continuing when I feel so badly. I have mixed feelings about stopping the chemotherapy. Part of me wants it to be over with, and to start feeling better, but part of me questions whether missing the last two treatments will have a negative impact on the progress we are making. I feel like somewhat of a failure because of not being able to see it through to the end. I guess I should put it in God's hands, and trust this decision is in my best overall interest.

In October, my sister and I are going to Costa Rica. This will be our third year doing a trip together, and I am excited. I must rebuild my stamina and strength since I challenged Nancy to ride a zip line while we are there. Dr. Fojo has requested a video of that experience.

## My "Opportunity to Excel"
### *Wilson Family Christmas letter*
### *(Chuck)*

Since the *Wilson Family Christmas Letter* is by no means an annual (or, when it does happen, an on-time occurrence) I was feeling no pressure. "Was" is the operative word here since the boss, Debbie, called me into her office the day after Thanksgiving for my preliminary *Annual Husbandly Performance Review*. This is much less formal than the official review; suit and tie were supposed to be optional. She provided a quick rundown of my noteworthy accomplishments so far, this *2012 Husband Year*:

- placed trash at curb prior to arrival of garbage truck (frequently)
- trimmed overgrown bushes (finally)
- improved personal hygiene (slightly)

Was then offered the opportunity to improve in an additional evaluation category before the end of the assessment cycle (the thirty-first of January). I reviewed the binder entitled *Elements of Husbandly Performance* for ideas.

Imagine my excitement as I perused the catalog of my shortcomings for ideas. I was careful not to overreach as I fear being labeled an *overachiever*. Long before the appendices, I made my selection: "Regularly fails to complete "Wilson Family Christmas Letter" before Christmas—if at all."

"That's it! That's my opportunity to excel!" I squealed.

"I was hoping you would select that one," Debbie said with a self-satisfied smile.

"Well, it was highlighted in yellow, and underlined in red," I observed.

"Oh, was it?" she said. Then she provided needed direction: "This year, I want our letter to be less ho-hum, hum-drum. We need to get with the times. I'm thinking something edgier, sort of a Santa reboot."

"Reboot Santa?" I questioned, trying to get a chuckle, but she was on a roll.

"Yes, reboot means to take something old, and give it a fresh updated look; like they've done with Batman, Spiderman...James Bond 007. Where have you been? Look at what currently passes for sophisticated; apply it to *our* family. Submit your rough draft A.S.A.P. Dismissed."

This morning (Christmas Eve) I was asked, "How's the letter coming?"

"Letter? ...oh, the letter. Great! Uh, just a few gritty-edgy details to go," I said, smiling a bit too much.

"It had better be in my hands by close of business," she said Clint Eastwood-style through clenched teeth.

There's nothing like a thinly veiled threat of certain violence to motivate a man.

### *Wilson Family Christmas Letter*

Yo, yo, y'all—it's Christmas!

Sure do hope you are not too shocked receiving this Christmas letter during the actual holiday season (was recently informed that the "holiday season" does not include Easter). Strange as it may sound, we are celebrating the way normal people do this year—that is, we are gathered round our hearth, and Christmas evergreen—versus Debbie in a hospital bed decorated with multiple IVs, and blinking medical monitors. It just doesn't feel like Christmas without major surgery. We're looking for a support group for people who don't have any problems.

It has been a year jam-packed with tremendous highs, and terrible lows. The toughest was losing my brother, Harry, to pancreatic cancer in February. Our paths crossed with Harry and Rose regularly at NIH where he and Debbie happened to share some of the same doctors. Such coincidences have delivered our greatest blessings. By chance, Debbie, and I were at NIH for scans the day Harry was discharged, and sent home to hospice care. Our last "goodbye, I love you brother," still hangs in the air. Later that same day, scans revealed a tumor the size of an orange in Debbie's liver. Still have a missed call message from Harry on my cell phone—left a few days before he was no longer able to speak. He was inquiring as to how his fellow cancer warrior, Debbie, was doing. Harry and Debbie were tremendous supporters of each other, communicating on a level few of us will ever understand.

Debbie underwent chemotherapy to treat that tumor with little expectation of the success we achieved. The tumor has reduced in size, and grows fainter with each scan since finishing treatments in July. She especially credits her faith in God, and close relationship with her oncologist Dr. Tito Fojo (her doctor since 2004), and his research nurse, Maureen Edgerly, as the reasons she is still alive. Debbie and Tito never part without a hug, and an "I love you." Doesn't everyone get that kind of treatment from their doctor?

I have been busy protecting the world from enemy submarines. Debbie's good health has allowed me to once again travel the planet. Just returned from South Korea the other day. During diplomatic drinking games at a dinner, I was told by a Republic of Korea naval officer (through an interpreter) that I look like a prototypical, iconic American—akin to a Santa Claus. Then, in the name of world peace, I proposed toasts to each of Santa's eight reindeer. It put them all under the table—which was not far to go since we were seated Native-American-style on the floor in our *stockings*.

Required Christmas letter fodder:

- In September, we rented a cottage for two weeks on Keuka Lake (in upstate New York) near where we grew up, met, fell in love, and got married. The first week, our sons, daughters-in-law, and granddaughters were there with us at what the little girls called "Papa's Lake-house." We had a blast navigating the lake in "Papa's Party Boat," riding in a hot-air balloon (owned by our friends, Kris and Becky Goodrich), enjoying visits from New York friends and family, and taking nostalgic road tours. We drove everyone to the rim of crazy with stories and points of interest, including the site of our first kiss in the parking lot of Pudgie's Pizza in Bath (there really should be a historic marker). The second week we spent with some of our old Iowa crew: Ron & Mardi Burmeister, and Rick & Susan Stacy. Boat rides, winery tours, lakeside bonfires, and a hike through the gorge at Watkins Glen were highlights.

- To celebrate our thirty-fifth anniversary, we renewed our vows at Keuka College Chapel (where we were married). Roxanne Von Hagn arranged it, and Rick Stacy officiated. Also in attendance were Debbie's cousin Lorraine, and her husband Gerhard König, Milt Von Hagn, and Susan Stacy. Got so choked up after hearing the nice things Debbie had to say about me (believe it or not), was nearly unable to read my comments about her.
- Debbie visited Costa Rica in October with her sister, Nancy. They even zip-lined through the rainforest.
- Completed a paver-patio project in our backyard including a gas fire pit, and hot tub (woo-hoo!).

Thank God for the blessings he has poured on us this year. We're especially thankful to have both of our sons living nearby with their wonderful wives, and beautiful daughters. Addison (three), and Aubrey (two-and-a-half) bring us great joy. Baby Layla is due to arrive in March. All are doing very well, by the way.

Y'all have a yo-yo merry, edgy, gritty Christmas overflowing with love, and peace from the one for whom the season is named.

Blessings from the whole dang Wilson family,
Debbie and Chuck

Well, I turned in my assignment (above) with seconds to spare. The boss read it; think I saw the welling of a tear at one point, and the start of a smile at another.

Then, Debbie said, "Well, it's pretty good, but a bit too corny, and it needs editing. First, it's too long—*nobody* will read it! Also, I'm not sure it's a good idea to mention your reindeer drinking games with the Koreans. Isn't that a state secret?"

I sure hope our "Wilson Family Christmas Letter" goes out on time this year—got a lot riding on it. Maybe I'll throw in some vampires or zombies; they're popular. The best thing is, even if it gets sent out late, it won't be my fault...hmm, at least I hope not. I mean, how could it be my fault? Anyway, I'll read about it in my official *2012 Annual Husbandly Performance Evaluation*.

# CHAPTER 12

# OF ANNIVERSARIES
# AND AFFAIRS

*(Debbie)*

It's 2014. Well, it appears that change is the only constant. Heraclitus, a Greek philosopher, said, "The one thing in life you can absolutely count on is that circumstances will continually change. The great unknown is when they will change."

(First, if I were him, I would have changed my name!)

I have a new cancer. Chronic lymphocytic leukemia with small cell lymphoma (CLL/SCL). A CT scan last October revealed enlarged lymph nodes in the back of my abdomen. Biopsies were performed, but were inconclusive so the research doctors did some additional stains. As it turns out, those lymph node biopsies and my recent blood tests are consistent with a chronic lymphoma—the lymphoma is basically spilling into my blood.

I was referred to the head of the lymphoma clinic at NIH. His assessment was that many people live with CLL a long time before their symptoms need to be addressed. He feels we should not do anything right now—just continue to monitor the disease through blood analysis.

Now to the rest of the story: there are about five lesions in my lungs. One was biopsied and determined to be adrenal cortical cancer (one of the original cancers I've fought for about the last twenty-five years; that sucker keeps rearing its ugly head). It is assumed the other four lesions are also adrenal cancer. It's funny; I feel well. I have no complaints other than occasional fatigue, and sometimes shortness of breath. I attributed both to not getting enough exercise.

So, the plan has changed to more chemotherapy to beat back the tumors. Once I accepted the reality of it all, we decided to move ahead as quickly as possible. It was arranged through my NIH oncologist and Dr. Tann, my local oncologist, to undergo treatment in Chesapeake—the same place I had my last chemotherapy regimen.

So here I am again with my Kindle, my knitting, and my bottled water. They drew my blood, and sent me back to the recliner of my choice. I'm trying to keep busy with projects, though I find I get tired easily. I'm anxious to get these treatments done so we can get back to our house projects. We just finished painting the kitchen and living room. Chuck did most of the work; I taped the trim. He also painted the ceiling in both rooms. I bought some fabric to make Roman shades for the kitchen; another project to complete. I'll have to organize my sewing room to have space to work, so it's time to get on with (and get over) chemo.

### (Chuck)

Two days after Debbie began chemo, we found ourselves in the Chesapeake Hospital Emergency Room. She was experiencing chest pain that could have possibly indicated a pulmonary embolism. Scans showed the pain was not an embolism, but due to enlarged lymph nodes (irritated by the chronic lymphocytic leukemia), the constant coughing, and possibly an infection. Things did not improve over the following days as she ran fevers as high as 102.1 degrees, continued to cough, and developed mouth sores from the chemo.

After hearing about what she was going through, her medical team at NIH asked us to drive up immediately. They compared the most recent scan (taken while she was in the ER) to the scan taken in February. The comparison showed significant growth (twenty to twenty-five percent) in the adrenal carcinoma lung tumors since her last scan in February—just two months ago. They also conducted a bronchoscope which showed one lobe of her left lung to be completely blocked by a tumor.

We have been sensing for a while that things are not going well. Our fears were confirmed during a meeting with her NIH medical team.

We gathered in an examining room with two of her doctors and her nurse coordinator. They informed us, in what can only be described as the most sensitive and loving way possible, that Debbie's disease has moved into a new phase. There are no longer any "hit it out of the park" options available in the cancer-fighting arsenal. We have moved into the "deal with the symptoms" phase. The "keep her comfortable" phase.

It was also recommended we consider the H-word: hospice. We were assured there is nothing imminent. However, Debbie was gently informed that now is a good time to focus on being at peace with her life.

In other words, she was told, once again, to get her affairs in order.

This time, without any tears, Debbie said, "I am not afraid to die."

She is, however, concerned about controlling the pain, but does not want to go out as a drugged-out zombie. She wants to be aware to the end, and experience her passing in the arms of her family with as much grace as she can muster.

Since that meeting, we have been staying busy, doing our best to outrun the anxiety we have in tow, while coming to terms with the new realities of Debbie's medical situation. We are both a bit numb right now, but are floating on our faith, and the prayers of our friends and family.

Debbie is the most remarkable person I have ever known. Her inner strength seems to grow as her physical strength is challenged. I love her more each day.

### (Debbie)

So, let me explain how I see things at this point. There is serious business going on in my lungs—I saw the picture of the blocked bronchial tube. It's scary, but we are hoping the chemotherapy will shrink the tumors. There are options, including laser technology, and stents to open the airway if the chemotherapy doesn't work.

Right now, I am about the business of living as best as I can—not dying. We will all die one day, but as far as I know, there is no expiration stamp anywhere on my body that says I'll be leaving anytime soon.

When I get the word that nothing more can be done to treat the symptoms or keep me comfortable, I plan to be in control of my passing, living each day with joy. In the meantime, I intend to spend as much time as possible with my family, laughing, reminiscing, and making some new memories. I don't want to be enveloped in a cloud of morose, sad feelings. For now, I have made the decision to live, and will do it the best way I know how, surrounded by those I love.

As for my relationship with God, and my faith walk, I have complete trust in what God has planned for me. God didn't plan for me to have cancer, it just happened. People get sick no matter what their level of faith is.

It's a beautiful day, and I'm sitting on my sunporch sipping my first cup of coffee in over a month. Chuck is mowing the lawn, and everything about today feels and smells like June, and summer, and home.

I had two amazing surprises for my birthday. First, my friend Mattie Rhoades Haines showed up from Oregon. She is the owner of a company named Quiltsmart and had been doing a quilt show in Pittsburgh, and called to see if she could somehow visit me while on the east coast.

As much as I wanted to see her, I didn't want her to go to the trouble of adding on a trip to Virginia. We agreed we would get together at the end of the summer. I was stunned when she showed up late one night a couple days before my birthday. She had found a flight to Richmond, then rented a car and drove to Chesapeake. Wow. She has so much energy, and enthusiasm.

Before I knew it, Mattie, my daughter-in-law Jen, and I were working on those Roman shades I vowed to complete months ago. We made seven shades, and put them up. Had a few minor issues with a couple of them (glue showing through the fabric), so Mattie cut and prepared two extra panels to replace the defective shades. I'm simply happy to have them finished and installed.

For my birthday, Mattie, Jen, my granddaughter Addison, and I spent the day shopping, going out to lunch, and ended up at a fabric store when I got a call from Chuck. He seemed anxious for us to get home so we nixed our plan to visit the beach, and headed directly back to Chesapeake. Imagine my shock when my friend, Roxanne, popped out of a hiding place, and yelled, "Surprise!" What a great birthday it was.

Mattie had to return to Oregon the following day, but Roxanne stayed on. We had a wonderful time. We spent a day at the beach, and enjoyed our few days together. Roxanne stayed long enough to go with me to my third chemotherapy treatment, which puts me at the halfway point in my chemo schedule.

While it was a fabulous birthday week, chemotherapy ended the fun by knocking me for a loop. I started feeling sick the evening of my treatment, and it got worse each day. The infusion was on a Tuesday, and by Sunday I was so miserable I thought I would have to go to the ER.

Chuck had gone to church, and I was lying in bed miserable and teary when my friend, Felicia Proud, called to check on me. She suggested I get some Gatorade and Imodium. I hadn't been able to eat or drink much for days so it made sense that I was likely dehydrated, and in need of fluids. I followed her advice, and within hours of forcing myself to get the Gatorade down (plus one Imodium), I began to feel a little better.

I cried a lot Sunday and Monday and don't know why. I just felt so defeated, weak, and so discouraged. Missing my mother, I ended up calling my Aunt Kay, her sister, the next best thing to talking to my mom. Then, yesterday it was as if a switch had been flipped, and I felt much, much better. I cooked, and ate a meal last night, and it tasted good. The mouth tenderness is there, but I don't have the horrible mouth sores I had the first couple of treatments.

This morning Addison and I sat on the sunporch listening to the song, "Happy," bouncing along to the beat. I can't believe how much better things look today. Feeling weak, but seeing a light at the end of the tunnel. It's easy to be positive when I feel better. It's those dark moments when I find my faith; my perseverance is so challenged, but then God sends reassurance through the kind actions of friends and family. I feel blessed to be so loved.

How many people have *angels* who drive hours and hours to spend time with them? My family and friends consistently check in with me, encourage me, listen to me share my deepest fears and concerns.

Dear Friends and Family,

Chuck and I are writing this together, as we have some difficult news to share. Due to the realities of my medical situation, I have decided to cease all cancer treatment.

Please know I would not be doing this if there were any viable means to continue the battle. To date, I have undergone four out of six possible chemotherapy treatments. Today was to be my fifth. However, yesterday I underwent scans at NIH which revealed the chemotherapy is not working. The tumors in my lungs have grown.

We spoke at length with my medical team, and further treatment of any sort would cause more harm than good. There are simply no good options. My body is not up to the demands of the even more toxic treatment options available. Besides, there is virtually no chance of benefit anyway. I would suffer awful side effects for nothing.

We are all disappointed, but Chuck and my doctors are totally supportive of my decision to cease treatment. I prefer to embrace life as long as I can, feeling as well as possible. Chemotherapy made me very, very ill with numerous debilitating side effects. Continuing, knowing it is not working, makes no sense.

My NIH oncologist believes I will feel better as soon as the toxicity of the chemotherapy works its way out of my system. He predicts the next three months will have me feeling quite well before the disease impacts my health. He also says I have a significant portion of healthy lung remaining. In two to three months, we will go back to NIH to be scanned again, and my medical team will assess where I stand.

I didn't ask for, and don't want, a prediction of how long I have before the disease gains control. I don't believe my doctor would even try to answer that question, anyway. He has encouraged us to travel and visit friends and family as soon as possible.

"Do not delay!" he emphasized.

The goal at this point is to keep me comfortable—I have no pain as of this posting, but do have an annoying cough, which is being treated with a low dose of liquid morphine. The team recommended I begin a relationship with a local hospice organization to assist in monitoring my medical situation, and to provide support for my family.

It's all been a lot to digest, but I knew this day would come. My hope is I can face this phase of my life with grace, and peace of mind. We are packing the next few months with travel including a Disney trip with the kids and grandkids.

Who knows, I may surprise everyone, including the doctors at NIH, and hang in there for a long time. Next week we travel to upstate New York to visit friends, and family. I am also attending my fortieth high school class reunion. I want this to be a time of laughter, reminiscing, and celebration, *not* doom and gloom.

That said, please continue to pray for us. I'm not afraid, and don't want anyone to be sad. I've been blessed with a great life—even the past twenty-seven years since my first diagnosis. I have been able to see my children grow, and have children of their own...and I plan to make some great memories in the upcoming months.

Love,
Debbie

# CHAPTER 13

# THE HAMMOCK

### *(Debbie)*

I t has been three months since my medical team at NIH told me to begin a relationship with hospice, and "consider life in three month increments." I am happy to report I am still around, and considering my next three months

My NIH team also advised me to plan, and do whatever travel I might want to accomplish "sooner rather than later." Also, they believed I would enjoy relative good health for a while once the effects of the chemo wore off. My subsequent trip to upstate New York was cut short a few weeks later—just shy of attending my fortieth high school class reunion—when my left lung decided to collapse. That experience, and the ensuing complications made me especially anxious about my chances of accomplishing our planned Disney trip. I am so thankful my time at Disney World went so well.

That brings me to thoughts about my life for the next three months. This process involves a reassessment of where I now stand physically:

- It is challenging to balance the use of medications for pain, and insomnia with the need for clarity of thought.
- There have been many days when I have needed to sleep about twenty out of twenty-four hours.

- I am often very unstable on my feet, and have fallen several times (including a few times out of bed). Chuck insists I wake him before getting up in the night. I now have a "rollator" (a glorified walker with wheels, handbrakes, a seat for when I get tired, and a compass in the stock—a reference to Ralphy's Red Ryder BB-Gun in *Christmas Story;* I love that movie).
- There is a wheelchair in the dining room I refuse to use.
- My interest in sewing, knitting, reading, going for walks or venturing anywhere is much diminished.
- Because of my frequent spills, Chuck has taken to giving me my drinks in the sippy-cups we have around the house for our granddaughters.
- I use oxygen when sleeping.
- I battle a chronic cough, fever, and my blood pressure has been high (although today it was low).

As you can see, my independence, personality, and pride are under assault.

I'm blessed to have family, and friends, near, and far, who call me, send cards, and even come to see me. A group we met while living in Iowa came for five days, and cooked meals to freeze for later use. When they weren't cooking, we played cards, and reminisced. I didn't have to lift a finger while they were here. My sister, Nancy, emails me a *sister moment* every day, sharing her love, and special thoughts. Friends drove all the way from Tennessee for a three-hour visit. My brother, Gary, and most of his family came for a weekend, and MaryAnn made her famous lasagna, and eggplant parmesan. I could mention so many who have lifted me up, and supported me, but it would be a never-ending list. All I can say is, "thank you" from the bottom of my heart.

What's left to do? I've done most of the things I need to do to get my affairs in order, including training Chuck to pay the bills. This task has become much easier as nearly everything is set up to be paid automatically. We even met with a Funeral Director the other day to discuss final arrangements—that was a strange experience. Chuck found my desire to stop at Dairy Queen for my usual small soft-chocolate cone after discussing my cremation especially surreal. I have only two outstanding tasks: selecting pictures for a slideshow for my memorial service, and writing my obituary. I have selected the songs, but still need to go through our many pictures. I have retained final approval authority for those projects—gotta be in control of something.

I watch the news most every day. The world seems to be falling apart faster than I am. I enjoy watching *Jeopardy*, and *Wheel of Fortune*. They remind me of my mother. There are a few new television series I like: *Justified*, *The Knick*, and *Gotham*. My all-time favorite series remains *Breaking Bad*. There are so many great shows, right now. I also spend a lot of time with investigative documentaries about various homicides playing back-to-back as I pass in and out of sleep. Why does such stuff relax me?

The next three months include the holidays, and I so want to make them extra special for my family. I have good days, and bad days so it will be a challenge to make that happen. Fortunately, I know my sons, and daughters-in-law will pitch in to help.

Love to all,
Debbie

### (Chuck)

"Can I have another blanket?"

"Of course," I say. "Any preference?"

"Yes, that ugly afghan my mother made for me with all of the crazy colors."

"You got it, babe."

In an instant, I rise from the Adirondack chair next to the hammock, and stop providing the impetus for the easy rocking motion. Debbie is already cocooned beneath two quilts. Sam Smith is singing to us from my Bose Bluetooth speaker on the table a few feet away. We love Pandora, and the music selections that come up on our chosen stations. I can't stand to leave her for even a moment now without a touch of some kind. Her sweet face smiles up at me as I bend to kiss her forehead.

"Thank you for never giving up on me; for never letting me give up."

She is completely at peace with where she is—on the brink of death.

"You're welcome, babe," I say. "I wish you didn't have to leave me. I wish we could be together, forever."

"We will be," she says. "I don't want to leave you, but I don't have anything left. I must go. I am ready to go."

"I know, babe. This sucks," I say with the best smile I can muster, just as I have been saying the past few months since we conceded the battle-field to the unstoppable advance of cancer.

"It sucks big time," she replies with a smile so sweet I imagine a tooth-ache. I can hardly keep my balance. "You have to promise me you will be okay when I'm gone."

"I promise to be okay."

It's a lie—a lie I have lied countless times to her repeated request these past weeks. Her once dark brown eyes have softened. Her face melts me, like butter left out in the sun. I give the hammock one more gentle push, and turn toward the steps from our patio into the house. Tears race down my face. The thing is, I know I must make good on that promise even though I swear I am lying every time she makes me say it. Why does that make sense to me?

I am angry at God as I retrieve the heavy afghan from amongst the other handmade creations on the quilt rack. "Lord, why can't I just keep taking care of her? Why does this battle have to end? I thought we were your living examples of the power of faith; that we were supposed to show that cancer can be defeated...that giving up guarantees defeat so we should never give up...that if we don't concede, surrender, there's always a way forward. What the f***k, God?"

I compose myself, and wipe my face before stepping back out onto the patio. It is a gorgeous late autumn day in Chesapeake, Virginia, with temperatures in the mid-sixties. The leaves are gone, giving us signifi- cant access to cloudless blue. Clumps of pine branches, loaded with cones, sway back and forth atop the massive trees towering high over us. Debbie awakens as I place her mother's afghan over her. She sleeps most of the time, now.

"Thank you, honey," she says.

"You are very welcome, my dear," I reply.

Large blocks of orange, red, pink, yellow, green: yarn from sweaters my mother-in-law, Shirley, had made and torn apart due to ill-fit. Repurposed, remade, reborn yarn, the fiber of the ugliest afghan of all time. Shirley knew full well how god-awful it looked. She had a great sense of humor. Debbie is even funnier.

I try to count how many years it has been since Shirley passed. Five, six maybe? It was the year before we moved from Florida; the same year our sons both got married—after Brian's wedding and before Greg's. I should be able to remember this—figure it out. Debbie experienced the worst grief imaginable. I had never seen anything like it. She was on the front end of yet another cancer battle, lymphoma I think, when we received word of Shirley's passing. She sobbed night and day for weeks. I feared for her wellbeing as the mourning process dragged her to the bottom. How will I handle it—the grief—when Debbie passes? Will the emptiness swallow me? Will I let it? What possible reason will ever cause me to rise in the morning or go to bed at night; what pos- sible purpose?

"Are you sure you don't want to go inside where it's warm?" I ask.

"No, I want to be out here. I love our patio. I'm so glad we had this built. It's shaped like a piece of one of those jigsaw puzzles we used to work on at your grandmother's house. I feel like it represents where we are right now. We are trying to make sense of how this piece fits into the puzzle of our lives," she says, and pauses.

"I like that visual," I respond. "If God or someone perched in the top of one of these pines were to look down at us, and if all the other pieces of our lives were spread out around the neighborhood, would they be able to put everything together into a complete picture?"

"I'm sure God already has it figured out," she says. "Tell me your theory, again."

"My theory?"

"The one about heaven being independent of space and time. It gives me comfort."

"Oh, that theory. Didn't realize you were even listening when I told you about it. Figured you found it silly. Anyway, it's just food for thought. Don't put any stock in it."

"Shut up, and tell me, again. I only have so much time." She smiles, and gives me her "just do it" look.

"Okay, let's see, the Bible says God knows everything that has, and ever will, happen. He is the beginning, and the end, the Alpha and Omega. That means God created the universe knowing the full story. To him, the fullness of time from the big bang to a stone-cold universe happened and was fully realized by him. Created as a necessary expression of God's need to love; his need for relationship. We are limited to perceiving things as per the time-space continuum God created to make the universe possible.

"So, if God is independent of the time-space continuum, and that place, if it can be thought of as a place, is heaven, then we as humans are incapable of fully comprehending God or heaven. It is simply too outside our experience. Further, if we are ever going to exist in a heaven that is independent of space, and time, then as far as God is concerned, we already exist there with him. Everyone who has or ever will exist on the time-space continuum, if they are destined for heaven, is already there. I'm sure I'm not explaining it very well, and God is probably laughing at me, but..."

"Do you think Greg and Jen will have another child?" she asks.

"I hope so, but who knows?"

"I need to finish knitting that baby blanket, just in case. I like to think I will meet at least one unborn grandchild in heaven."

"That would be cool. So, if you and I are already there, we might be looking down on ourselves, sitting here on this puzzle-piece shaped patio, smiling."

"Perhaps," she says, "but I don't think I will be smiling at everything I have done. I have a lot of regrets."

"Maybe it's grace that lets us accept our humanness, our failings during our association with time and space. Without the grace of God, without the ability to forgive ourselves, we might exist independent of time and space, but our experience would be hell instead of heaven."

"I wish I had saved myself for you. I wish you had been my first, and only," she bemoans.

"Debbie, please stop beating yourself up for that. That was before we even met. You were young, and curious."

"I so wish I had been a better mother to our sons," she continues, "and a much better wife to you. I'm so sorry for all I have put you through. What kind of life have you had with me, sitting in hospitals, taking care of me hand-and-foot? You deserved better."

"Deb, stop. I would not trade our lives together for anything. You are a wonderful wife and mother. I love you with all I've got. I would be nothing without you, and the good, the bad, and the ugly stuff we have been through together. I would have no faith without you."

"I regret I was not more patient with the boys growing up. I wish I had been more supportive of the things you wanted to do. I held you back from so many things. I made your life hell because I was afraid."

"You did not keep me from doing anything. That was on me, I held myself back. I should have done a better job of including and working with you on what I wanted to do."

"Okay, but I was always too scared to take risks, to let you chase your dreams. I wasn't built for that like you are. I wanted you to take the safe route; live a simpler life. Promise me, and promise yourself you will become the writer you have always wanted to be."

"I promise."

"Without your constant encouragement, I would never have finished college, become a teacher, and survived cancer for twenty-eight years."

"Well, I am trying to find fault with your argument, but I have to concede. You are correct, I'm pretty wonderful."

"And humble, your favorite thing about yourself."

We laugh.

"I am so thankful I was able to do the Disney trip. I sure hope the two older girls will have memories of that trip," she says.

"We will all work to keep those memories alive," I promise.

"The day the two older ones were made into princesses at Bibbidy Bobbidy Boutique was my favorite part."

"That was fun. Addison and Aubrey were absolutely beaming," I say.

"I could not have done it if not for the scooter. Some days I could barely get out of bed. Thank you for taking such good care of me and always being so patient."

"My pleasure, my dear."

"Do you forgive me for my shortcomings?" she asks.

"Of course, I do. Do you forgive me for the times when I was impatient with you, for my poor business decisions that nearly ruined us?"

"Yes, I forgive you. You made more wise decisions than bad. If I had been more supportive, things could have gone so much better. We have become so much more because of our mistakes."

"Yes, sticking together through the tough stuff and the stupid stuff has blessed us, I think, with a level of love few experience."

"Yes, God granted me much more time than I could have ever hoped for, and blessed me with a loving husband who I love more every day. I love you."

"I love you, too."

We pause, and look up at the sky. Squirrels chatter in the trees, warning each other of a cat skulking through the woods. A group of large birds circling to the east resemble a cyclone.

"Aren't those buzzards?" Debbie asks.

"Yeah, I wasn't going to mention them."

"Ha, at least they aren't circling directly over me."

We both laugh, and continue looking skyward. A song "Lucky" plays on the Bose.

"I want this song in my Celebration of Life video. It reminds me of us. So, it's this song, 'Brown Eyed Girl' by Van Morrison, and 'You Can Count on Me' by Bruno Mars. I have it all written down in my Celebration of Life folder."

"I know," I say.

"And I don't want everyone sitting around all sad at my service. Although I do want everyone to laugh, and cry; experience the full range of emotions. I want it to be a celebration. Okay?"

"Yes, dear."

"Ha. Don't 'yes, dear' me."

"Yes, my queen."

We laugh.

"I guess I always assumed I would be in constant tears at this point, and need the minister here every day," she says. "I feel like all of the years facing cancer helped me develop the faith to get through this."

"Some folks would have themselves surrounded by crystals, pyramids or crucifixes," I offer.

"I just want my family with me when I go."

"I should have somehow bought the marijuana you wanted. It might help with the pain and increase your interest in eating."

"Yeah, but I don't want it now. I can't bear the thought of us getting arrested."

"Ha. Yeah, that would add an interesting twist to the book."

"Hotel California" is playing on the Bose. We listen as the guitars sing.

"I want a glass of wine with you, later," she says.

"We do serve that spirit here, but in a sippy cup, for you. Don't want to clean up another spill."

"I know, I can't control my arms very well anymore. They just fall. Sorry about the cranberry juice. That was awful. I make so much extra work for you."

"No worries. I'm happy to clean up after you."

"Thank you for taking such good care of me. You never complain. What would I do without you?"

"You will never find out."

I feel her forehead. She is running a temperature.

"I had better get the thermometer," I say, and start to rise.

"Don't bother. I'm okay. Besides, there is nothing to be done about it. I want you here next to me."

"Okay," I say, not wanting to ever leave her.

"I'm so glad we went to Prince Edward Island when we had the chance a few years ago. Promise me you will encourage our granddaughters to read the *Anne of Green Gables* books, watch the movies, and take them there, someday."

"I promise."

"Remember when we used to read William Faulkner books to each other?"

"Yeah, remember how we would read for a while, and then make love. Reading aloud was an aphrodisiac for us."

"I hate that my body became so misshapen by all of the cancer surgeries. I appreciate so much that you always made me feel desirable, even when I didn't have any hair, even after my breasts were removed."

"I always see you as that girl in the white veil, standing at the back of the church, ready to walk down the aisle to me. We've had a wonderful life together, despite the cancer. In some ways, I think the cancer made our love stronger. It sure helped us develop a strong faith."

"Yes, there was good that came about because of the cancer, but it still sucks that it's all coming to an end."

"It sucks, big time," I say.

"I love this spot. Our own Garden of Eden. Do you think there was a real Garden of Eden?" she asks.

"I don't know. Maybe. Probably based on something real. We don't have to believe in the Garden of Eden story or the Noah story to believe in God. I do think those stories were inspired, and meant to convey understanding of our relationship with God."

"Well, I will soon know the truth," she smiles as she says this.

"Bohemian Rhapsody" begins to play.

"Tell me your story about this song, again," she asks.

"Ha, the one when I was in South Korea?"

"Yeah, I love that story."

She looks at me, smiling. I lean over her, placing her in my shadow, and give her a kiss. Her fever is getting worse.

"Okay, so I was in South Korea again for another planning conference. As usual, the active duty officer and I were invited to one of those places where you sit on the floor and grill meat in front of you while drinking toast after toast to each other —through an interpreter. The South Koreans are wonderful hosts, and they love to get you drunk. I was always careful to make sure everyone participated in every toast so as to keep a level playing field. If you let them tag-team you, they will get you wasted. Anyway, since I was so much bigger than them, if we all drank the same amount, they would get drunk faster than me.

"When leaving the dinner, for some reason, we had to pack seven guys into a car built for five. It didn't bother me because I was the senior military officer, even though I was retired. That meant I rode shotgun in comfort in the front while five guys piled in the back on top of each other. The USN active duty lieutenant commander was a big guy, and he was jammed in back there, too. The four Koreans were small, but that is still a lot of guys in the back of a Hyundai.

"South Koreans love American music. They seem to know all the words, and love to sing along even though they may not understand English. When 'Bohemian Rhapsody' begins to play, everyone is singing at the top of their lungs. That's when this throbbing guitar piece starts, and, just like in the scene from *Wayne's World*, the head bobbing starts. I was dying laughing. When the song finishes, everyone holds that last note like Freddy Mercury. Then we all laugh.

"Through the interpreter, the lieutenant commander asks if they are familiar with the movie *Wayne's World*, because we had just reenacted a famous scene from it. They all claim to have not seen it, which made the whole episode that much funnier to us two Americans."

"You've sure done a lot of work around this place. Do you think you will stay here after I'm gone?" she changes the subject.

I'm stunned by the question. Debbie always has a way of surprising me. I think for a moment.

"I can't imagine not staying here. We did so much here, together. The kids and grandkids are nearby," I reply, searching for another answer I cannot find.

"The memories might make it hard for you to move on," she says.

"I…"

I find no ability to provide anything resembling a thoughtful response. The edge of nothingness is at my feet. I want to dive in.

"There is no marriage in heaven, you know," she says. "Do you think we will know each other there?"

I feel like I've sat down mid-semester in an upper level college class I have not attended to date, and have been asked a question by an esteemed professor. I steer into humor.

"Doesn't sound like heaven to me if we don't know each other. I also don't like it when people say there is no beer there. I mean, Whiskey Tango Foxtrot?!"

She smiles.

"I hate it when they say there is no sex there. No sex in heaven? That's B.S. The complaint department will be my first stop if that's the case."

The twinkle that is Debbie returns to her eyes. I bet her temperature is bumping into 102 degrees.

"We might go to hell for saying such stuff," I joke.

"As long as there's sex there!" she almost yells.

We both laugh, fully engaged in the goofy humor we have enjoyed together for so many years.

"The worst thing would be if we are expected to sing in the heavenly choir day in and day out," I complain.

"I'm quite certain you will not be a part of the heavenly choir. Pretty sure, though, they will put a lot of pressure on me to join," she says, making her usual mockery of my famous inability to carry a tune.

We laugh as if we have not a care in the world, certain God is laughing along with us but, like jumping out of an airplane without a parachute, it's the sudden stop that gets you. Reality hits.

"I am going to miss you, so much," I say as my throat swells, and the tears start to form.

"Don't cry. You can't cry," she insists. "You can cry after I'm gone, but right now I need you to be strong. I need you to be my rock!"

"Okay," I say, and get back into character.

"I want you to promise you won't sit around mourning too long before you begin exploring other relationships. Don't let anyone shame you into not seeing other women or that you have not waited long enough. Anyone who has observed us knows you have been a wonderful husband to me. You deserve happiness. Don't let anybody treat you bad. If they do, I will haunt them. Have several relationships, and find the person who will make you happy for the rest of your life, but don't forget me! Promise?"

"Forget who?" I pause for her come-closer-so-I-can-hit-you look. "Oh, like it would ever be possible to forget you. I wish we could trade places. I wish I could take your place, and you could live to a rich, old age, and die with blue hair on a beach in Florida while a couple of young dudes are applying suntan lotion to your wrinkled body."

She smiles.

"No, I'm the one getting off easy, here. I know you are going to go through hell. I could never handle it if you were the one to go first, and left me alone. You are the one built to handle what's coming, not me."

Looking up at the sky, I match the swing of the hammock to the back, and forth sway of the pinecone laden branches as they ride on the wind. Sam Smith is singing "Stay with Me."

"Do you think the love we have experienced is available to everyone?" she asks.

"I do, but both people in the relationship have to make that choice. We all have freewill. There also has to be forgiveness."

"Grace!" she inserts.

"Yes, a lot of grace."

Adele sings "Set Fire to the Rain."

"I think Adele and Sam Smith are two of the finest singers of all time."

"Me too. I don't understand people who refuse to listen to today's music. They are stuck in the fifties, sixties, or whatever decade. I think we are in a golden age of music and television series."

There is a bang on the porch window, and the door to the patio slides, and is left open.

"Mimi! Papa!" our oldest granddaughter, Addison, yells as she runs to us.

She gives me a hug, and then climbs into the hammock and under the blankets with her Mimi. She talks a mile a minute as Debbie asks her questions about her day, noses touching, eyes connected. Life could not be more perfect.

# CHAPTER 14

## A LITTLE BIT OF CHRISTMAS

*(Chuck)*

"I need to have a little bit of Christmas," Debbie announces to me from her La-Z-Boy recliner as I enter our family room. "Jen and I are going to Michaels to buy a new Christmas tree. There's a good one on sale. Seven-and-a-half feet tall, and pre-lighted..."

"The last pre-lit tree we bought was a piece of crap. Remember the section that stopped working an hour after we got it decorated?" I say.

"Yeah, but this one has good reviews online. I'm tired of the old one you haul out every year, and take four hours to put together, and get lighted exactly the way you like it. We've had that one for over twenty years, and it is falling apart. If this one goes bad, it will be your problem to deal with after I am gone. While we are out shopping, I want you to bring all of the Christmas stuff down from the attic."

The thought of all those trips to the attic, and transforming the house into Christmas Town is more than I am prepared for. I try one last appeal.

"But, Debbie, it's over two weeks until Thanksgiving! We always wait until after Thanksgiving to decorate for Christmas. Can't we wait for at least another week?"

"No. I don't know how long I have. I want a little bit of Christmas. Are you going to help me?"

"Okay," I say. "Do you really want everything brought down?"

Dumb question.

"Yes. Everything. I want to do a full-blown decorating job. Put everything out this year. Be sure to set up the little Florida tree on the sunporch, and the granddaughter tree in the dining room. I will decorate those with the girls. I want to make as many memories of me for them as I can."

"I know, babe."

"I want the tree over here," she says, standing in front of the family room window, and circling her outstretched arms over an area that includes various pieces of furniture. "Same as last year—I like for the lights to be seen from outside."

"Okay."

She has a surprising level of interest and energy today. Her health has declined to the point where she often sleeps about twenty hours per day, and requires oxygen most of the time. I am in a tail-chase trying to keep up with her increasing need for oral pain medication. She is asking to be placed on a "pain pump." I know what that means.

"I am worried about you falling at the store. What if you need oxygen?"

"Quit worrying. I'll be fine."

"I should come with you."

"No, Jen can take care of me if I need help. You have a lot of work to do here. Do you have everything you need to make your famous shrimp pesto tonight?"

"Yes, picked everything up at the grocery store this morning," I respond.

Jen comes downstairs.

"Okay, let's go shopping! Let's spend some money!" Jen says, smiling at me with a devilish twinkle in her eyes.

"Yes," Debbie says. "Can't wait to come home, and show you how much money we saved."

Debbie is smiling, joking with Jen, and could be confused for a normal healthy person as they leave the house. I head for the attic to get started on my assigned tasks.

When they return, Debbie is beaming, and talking a mile a minute. Amazing—yesterday she did not get out of bed. She is pleased to see the entry area is now crowded with stacks of various plastic crates and boxes marked "Christmas." Family room furniture has been shifted to create space for the tree. Also, as ordered, the dining room and sunporch are each equipped with a three-and-a-half-foot artificial tree sitting on an appropriate table.

"You have been busy. Thank you for your hard work, honey. There is a bunch of stuff to bring in from the car. I picked up some gifts for the girls. Everything I bought was on sale. You are going to love this new tree. It should only take a few minutes to set up. Can't wait to see it."

She loves getting a good deal. Jen helps me carry the large box containing the tree and several other items into the house. Any notion of taking a break after busting tail all morning is extinguished. I begin assembly. She is right. This is the easiest tree to set up we have ever had. I plug it in. All the lights work!

"That looks so nice. I love it," she says. "I want to decorate all of the trees this afternoon. I'm looking forward to the crew all being here. Everyone loves your famous shrimp pesto. It will be fun. Oh, Erin is bringing the salad."

"Good, that will save me some trouble."

I have a few simple specialties I like to make, my *famous* shrimp pesto being one of them.

As always, the arrival of my grandchildren is a spectacular production. Addison is excited, and bouncing at the front door.

"How many minutes until they get here, Papa?"

Brian's family van arrives out front.

"They're here!"

Addison pushes open the front door, and runs out. The side door of the van slides open, and Aubrey pops out.

159

"Aubrey!"

"Addison!"

The cousins collide in a hug, squealing with delight, then turn and run in my direction. Standing in the middle of the sidewalk, I open my arms to receive Aubrey. She bypasses me on her way into the house.

"Mimi!" I hear Aubrey shout from inside.

I know Debbie is receiving a big hug. All in, I place all my hopes on Layla.

"Papa!" Layla says.

At least one granddaughter acknowledges me. Layla will turn two in March, and still needs some help climbing down from the van. Payoff! She gives me a quick hug before heading inside for the real action with her sister and cousin. I follow her up the front steps, and hold the door. Debbie is inside.

"Layla!"

"Mimi!"

She grabs hold of Debbie's legs for a moment then moves into the house, and up the stairs toward Addison's bedroom, and sounds of fun.

"Help me find the decorations for the little trees," Debbie says. "I think I put that stuff in that green tub with the red top last year."

I move some containers around, and lift the desired storage tub onto the piano bench. It feels like I am opening a treasure chest. Sure enough, the flamingo lights, real seashell, fake fish ornaments, and fishnet tree skirt are the bounty before us.

"Can you get the girls down here to help me decorate the trees?"

"Girls," I call up the stairs. "Addison, Aubrey, Layla, come on down, and help Mimi decorate the Christmas trees."

"Yeah," I hear.

A few big thuds and a prolonged crash, followed by running feet. What fell, I wonder? Would hate to look into that room, right now.

"Be careful, girls," I say, wasting my breath as Addison and Aubrey elbow each other in the side-by-side race down the stairs, and leap the last few steps onto the main floor at my feet.

"Out here, girls," Debbie says.

The headlong assault adjusts course without slowing. Back up the stairway, quick as she can, Layla is sliding down, one step at a time, on her butt. Emulating the big girls, she jumps from the last step. Leaning toward the sunporch, her legs scramble to keep up with her torso. Debbie is already attaching wire hangers, and handing out ornaments to her four-year-old granddaughters. Layla joins the bouncing bodies and upward-grasping hands.

As a second child, Layla's experience at our house is so different from that of Aubrey and Addison. An exploratorium, the older girls spent their visits to Mimi and Papa's finding, and experiencing the artifacts from our travels: the Chinese stress balls with the strange feel and inner jingle; the golf ball piggy bank filled with coins from around the world that was emptied—refilled, and emptied again—onto the floor every visit; the donning of ball caps from my various ships and shore commands; carvings of giraffes, gazelles, rhinos, elephants, Buddha, and a globe to find Antarctica, Australia, Italy (it's shaped like a boot), Japan, and Madagascar (where the animals sing the "Do It, Do It," song). Since Addison lives here now, Layla imposes herself on the older girls, and plays with Addison's mountain of toys.

Observing Debbie in her glory, her little girls dancing around her like she is a bonfire, I stand transfixed. The room is aglow with fleeting love and magic, like that optical moment just before the sun slips beneath the horizon. My heart flutters. Holding my breath, I try to hold onto the sight—the illusion. This sunset will never happen again.

What does Debbie want them to know and remember? That she loves them completely? What wisdom would she pass soul-to-soul for guidance as they live their lives?

- Rule One: Give life, and love all you've got.
- Rule Two: Do what is uncomfortable.
- Rule Three: Never be held to an unworthy situation or person.
- Rule Four: Never be an unworthy person.
- Rule Five: Do not allow yourself to be mistreated.

- Rule Six: You will be okay, no matter what.
- Rule Seven: Do not make promises lightly.
- Rule Eight: Do not be held to promises that will destroy you unless the cause is truly worthy.

What else would she want them to know? What else…?

I back out of the scene, smiling and tearing up. Behind me, Brian and Erin are also witnessing the perfection, and smile at me. They read my face. None of us can speak.

The decorating team completes the Florida tree, and moves to the dining room. The ornaments are small, specially framed Christmas pictures of the girls.

"Look how little I was in this picture," Addison says to Aubrey.

Layla is confused as to why she has fewer ornaments with pictures than the big girls.

I open the boxes of ornaments for the new main Christmas tree, and begin attaching wire hangers to get ahead of demand, or at least try. Debbie referees as the greedy little tree decorators snatch and argue over who gets to hang which ornament.

"Girls, there are plenty of decorations for everyone."

"I think it's time for some wine," I say.

Brian, Erin, Greg, and Jen chime in.

"Yes, this calls for alcohol," says Erin, feeling the emotion of the day, and as a way of dealing with the excited little girls.

"I'll have a rum and coke," Greg says.

"Pour me some, too," Debbie says.

"Okay, but in a wine sippy-cup," I say.

"My sister bought those wine sippy-cups for you because you were famous for pouring wine on yourself at parties," Debbie replies.

Everyone laughs at me.

"Okay, I've had my share of wine spills," I admit. "Those accidents all happened with my first glass of the evening."

Cabernet flows as I prepare dinner. Shrimp pesto is my favorite meal to prepare. My timing is perfect. Neither the noodles nor the shrimp are overcooked. Jen and Erin supplement my efforts in the kitchen. Brian, Greg, and Debbie are sitting together in the family room, enjoying the tree, their drinks, and each other. The bits and pieces of old stories I overhear bring full-blown memories to mind.

### Chuck's Famous Shrimp Pesto Recipe

Okay, so buy a pound of fettuccine or linguini, sixteen ounces of your favorite pesto (two 8.1 ounce jars of Classico Traditional Basil Pesto works great), a pound or so of raw large or jumbo shrimp, shredded or grated Parmesan, a deep bench of decent red wine, Caesar salad fixin's, and, totally optional, pine nuts. I don't usually bother, but they do add a nice bit of crunch. Plus, knowing those damn pine nuts cost about eighteen dollars per pound causes you to savor each bite a bit more. If granted this recipe as a last meal, request pine nuts.

First, open a bottle of wine to imbibe while cooking. Then, if you have not done so, thaw the shrimp in a colander under cold running water. This requires at least ten minutes so focus on consuming wine while performing this task. While it's a good idea to thaw the shrimp overnight in the refrigerator, I can count on one finger the number of times I've had the forethought to do so. If you are anxious, you might start the water toward boiling. Studied fingers can cause the fresh-thawed shrimp to slide from their outer covering naked, just like the mayor's daughter in *Animal House* slipping through the back of her prom dress. More wine.

When the water is at a rolling boil, like lovers under a blanket, tip in some extra virgin olive oil, and enough sea salt to rid your porch stoop of a horde of slugs. Believe me, watching slugs melt like the Wicked Witch of the West delivers a certain satisfaction. Then, and only then, take hold of a fistful of the finest noodles sold in your local market. Quality noodles are key. Do not even think about breaking them in half or dumping them directly from the package into the brine. Such actions are of a heathen worthy of the lash. Ease those noodles into the bubbling cauldron like a lineup of seated girls sliding from the pool's edge, legs-first into the water. Allow them to splay out, standing stiff around the pot like playing cards under a sharp's skilled hand. Patience. Take a few sips of wine. Now, without undue force, encourage acceptance of their fate as the hot penetrating moisture relaxes their rigid morals; allows them to bend, and become the free, and loose noodles they were meant by God himself to be.

Stir occasionally until 1-2 minutes before al dente done. It's time to dump the shrimp from the colander with a swirl, and the purging swift-ness required to empty the contents of a chamber pot out the window into the streets of sixteenth-century London. That's why men are sup-posed to walk on the street side of their dames, you know.

Without over cooking anything, drain, and add pesto, and nuts (optional). Stir, serve with wine, Caesar salad, and the best bread avail-able. Demand praise. After all, you just spent thirty minutes of your life preparing the feast.

Dinner with the granddaughters is always a challenging overlap-ping of processes. Adult courses are prepared as little girls are gathered under protest to the table. Mothers provide what their fussy progeny will eat. Addison is the fussiest. She survives on hotdogs, grilled cheese, Kraft mac-n-cheese (only Kraft), chicken tenders, PB&J, and chocolate milk. Aubrey and Layla are much better eaters at home, but the rules at Mimi and Papa's are lax, and the level of excitement always high. More food hits the floor for clean up by the dog, Barley, than makes its way into little bellies.

"Time for the blessing. Everybody, hold hands," I announce to the cross current of parents and children.

Aubrey wants to hold Addison's hand. Addison doesn't want her to. Layla does not want to participate at all. Somehow, the family-chain is formed.

"Father God," I begin, having no idea where I am going with the prayer. "Thank you for the blessings you pour on us, for this special day together. Be with us as we enjoy each other, tell old stories..." My voice fails me for a moment. "Bless this food to our bodies, and us to thy service. In Jesus' name, amen."

Aubrey is crying.

"I wanted to say the blessing," she whimpers.

"Okay, okay, everybody, hold hands again."

"God is good, God is great, and we thank him for our food, amen."

The melee recommences. The girls argue and whine to garner their favorite color sippy-cup, plate, spoon, and placemat. They each insist on spooning the powdered Nesquik into their milk. Pouring the milk, I try to limit the amount of chocolate reaching the floor for Barley, Greg and Jen's dog, to lap up. Chocolate's supposed to be bad for dogs. If that were true, every family dog we ever had would have been cut down in its prime.

Next, they wrestle for their desired chair, and complain they are not sitting next to whom they want to sit next to. Then, the realization dawns that they must have the placemat currently in front of another. After all of that, the chocolate milk their parents told them not to drink until after they have eaten is gone. Very little food is consumed. The two older girls are ready to leave the table. A futile effort by parents ensues, prevailing upon them to eat something. Parents capitulate. Addison and Aubrey scramble out of their seats, and thunder back upstairs to Addison's room to play. Not a single adult has yet sat down to the table. Layla asks for more olives. We all laugh.

"Those girls need to eat more," Debbie says.

"Leave their plates; they will return when they are hungry," Jen says.

Barley is licking the seats of their chairs clean. I take a long sip of wine.

"Yeah, I'm tired of fighting with them. I'm hungry, and would like some adult time. Sitting down to a nice meal, and a glass of wine, without being tugged on would be great," says Erin.

We finish filling plates and salad bowls, refill wine glasses, and take our seats. Debbie and I share a smile, as we twirl noodles and shrimp into the tablespoons I put out for everyone—but only she and I use. I'm pleased with the elements of the feast as I savor it. Sure am glad I added those pine nuts.

"Everything tastes great, Dad."

"Yeah, perfect."

"Thanks," I say.

Old stories flow with the wine.

After dinner Jen and Erin pitch in, helping me with clean up. Debbie goes into the family room with the boys, and continues decorating. The little girls are upstairs playing. Things might be a bit too quiet up there, but nobody wants to check on them. It's possible, after all, they are playing nice...would hate to disturb that.

"We will finish up here," Jen says. "Why don't you go in, and spend some time with Debbie and your sons?"

"Well, okay," I say, and join Debbie on the couch from where she is directing the boys. Shelves are emptied of the items normally there, and replaced with Christmas.

Memories pop into conversation as work continues.

Jen and Erin join us with restored glasses of wine, and everyone takes a seat.

"I have something important to say," Debbie begins. "There is something I need all of you to do for me."

We sense the gravity of her approaching announcement pulling us into a dark place.

"This will be hard for you to hear, but I have nothing left...I need for all of you to let me go."

Stunned, we sit silent.

"Your father is arguing with me about this, but I want the pain pump. I am ready for it. I need it. I can't go on like this. I can't do this anymore. This isn't living."

She has gone over my head to the voters. We are all unable to speak for what seems an eternity.

"You have to promise me that when the time comes," she continues, "you will not let me be in pain. That is the thing I fear most. I'm not afraid of dying. I'm ready to go. I do not want to be in pain...and I do not want to be alone. I want all of you with me when I die, but you must let me go. You have to pray for God to take me."

My mind is working through what she is saying, and evaluating where I stand. What is my opinion on the subject? She has endured too much for me to deny her this request. She has earned this act of respect. I must do as she is asking. Every part of me wants to stay in the fight, forever. This fight is all I know. Letting her go means she will, at some point soon, no longer be. I can't fathom the concept. Can't grok it. She is everything to me.

The room is overfull with heavy hearts and minds. No one wants to speak; to become part of this conversation. Our silence is not acceptable to Debbie.

"Brian, you are my oldest son. Will you let me go?"

Tears are welling in the eyes of our sons.

"I don't want to let you go, Mom...but I will," Brian chokes out.

"Greg, will you let me go?"

"Mom, you have outlived all expectations," Greg begins, with resolve. "All of your doctors are amazed at how long you have survived. I know this time is different. I can feel it. It breaks my heart you will not see Addison grow up."

He chokes and the tears flow.

"Chuck, will you let me go?"

Why is she asking me this? Why can't things continue as they are? I don't want to answer. Hours seem to pass. I am frozen in place. A response comes from a remote part of me. Words are coming out of my mouth. I listen as if someone else is speaking. A new part of me is stepping up to the plate. A pinch-hitter part of me is filling in, taking over.

"Debbie, you have fought long, and hard. We are all so proud of you. I hate this more than anything. There is no getting past the damn cancer this time. There are no good times on the other side of this one. You have earned the right to ask us to do this. There is no shame in letting yourself go. Not now. You are out of options. I love you with everything I've got. I would gladly take care of you, forever. I would trade places with you in a heartbeat."

"Will you let me go?"

"Yes, I will let you go. I mean it this time...I will make myself mean it, this time."

We all sit, and look at the tree, stockings hung from the mantle with care, ceramic Santas, crèche scene, Christmas village with cotton for snow, Christmas chessboard—our little bit of Christmas.

"Good. Now, I want to watch *A Christmas Story*. I want to hear Ralphy tell Santa he wants a Red Ryder BB gun, and for Santa to say, 'You will shoot your eye out, kid,' then put his boot on Ralphy's forehead, and push him down the slide. I want to watch our old Christmas videos from when you boys were little. I want a little bit of Christmas. I want you to all be happy when you remember me. I want those little girls to have good memories of me."

### Excerpt from Chuck's personal journal

November 15, 2014

I am in a constant state of anxiety; dread. I feel like I am wearing my clothes out from the inside due to my constant state of agitation. Debbie's appearance, pain level, blood pressure, temperature, and desires are all I consider; my only purpose is her existence. My heart is racing, and my breathing is shallow. I am being dragged into the future. A future I do not want. A future without Debbie.

November 22nd, 2014
Dear friends, and family,

First, I must apologize to so many of you for my slow reply to several calls and e-mails. My capacity for communication has been at an all-time low when I need it most. Debbie needs me immediately at hand at all times. She depends on me for everything. When I do have time between chores, my brain only wants quiet. I must wait for a wave to wash the energy and mental wherewithal ashore before I can pick up the phone or computer. I am hoping this will provide answers to many of your questions.

This past week, Debbie's condition worsened markedly. Last Sunday night she had an episode of momentary inability to breathe that caused her to have a panic attack. We have medications for that sort of thing, but on Monday a pain pump was installed by her hospice nurse providing a constant intravenous flow of Dilaudid. We have been using Dilaudid in pill and liquid form for some time to address her cough, breathing issues, and pain. Morphine is the drug of choice, as it works much better, but morphine always makes her sick; so Dilaudid it is. The flow rate for the Dilaudid has been increased twice already to keep up with symptoms. There is also a button we push for an extra dose when the going gets tough.

To be clear, we are in the "keep her comfortable" phase. The expectation is that over the coming days and weeks, the Dilaudid flow rate will be adjusted upward as needed until she is in a constant dream state (coma). Then, when she is ready, she will slip from this life with minimal distress.

A few weeks ago, Debbie decided to decorate for Christmas. She, in fact, went to Michaels with our daughter-in-law Jennifer, and bought a new Christmas tree—it looks great! This past weekend, her sister, Nancy, came for a visit. Debbie was very much looking forward to this visit, and it is likely no coincidence her decline began as Nancy's departure approached. They have the most wonderful sister relationship I have ever seen.

With Thanksgiving a few days away, our daughters-in-law, Erin and Jen, are taking up the cause. They have gone through Debbie's special recipes, and are preparing everything as she would have it, including cranberry, apple, and pumpkin pies. Greg is even deep-frying a turkey—our first ever! Debbie so wishes she could pitch in, and that our Canadian friend, Betty Jeanne Kippen, could also be here employing her pie-making skills.

I promise I am doing my best for her. She insists I remain strong as she needs me to be. So, like a good sailor, I am doing as told.

Reporting from the trenches,
Happy Thanksgiving to all,
Chuck

Thanksgiving week looms before us. On Monday, Debbie and I finished watching an episode of *The Knick*—a fascinating series. We enjoy shows with characters that are really "out there." Debbie is feeling talkative.

"I'm so glad Cliff and Edie, and Joe and Felicia made it down to see me. I still can't believe Brenda Wrather and Barbara Lakey drove thirteen hours from Covington, Tennessee to see me for three hours, and then turned around, and drove thirteen hours back home. And Roman, he flew here from Switzerland as soon as we told him I was on hospice care. It was so hard to say goodbye to him.

"There are so many people still wanting to come. I hate to say it, but I simply don't have the strength anymore. You must say no to everyone else. Call people, and let them know. Roxanne and Dolores want to come down. Also, your mom and Lorraine. I really feel bad, but I need to save my strength. I just can't rise to whatever occasion anymore."

"Okay, but you know how hard it is for me to say no."

"I love that about you, but you have to do this for me. You have to say no."

"Okay, babe. I will. I will be the defender at the walls. Nobody gets in. This sucks," I offer.

"Big time!" she replies.

Her tank is running on empty. So little of the old spark left. A wall is being built between us. Only her eyes remain in the space between the bricks.

"You have to maintain the traditions I have worked so hard to keep up for us all these years: birthday cards, annual Christmas letter...you have to stay on top of the bills. I've done my best to build and maintain our credit rating. Promise?"

"I will, I promise."

I feel the tears start to swell, but force the emotion down. I have no idea how I can carry on the stuff, the traditions, the attention to detail she is so good at.

Monday morning of Thanksgiving week, our hospice RN Monica arrives and checks Debbie's vitals. We have dealt with only two hospice nurses, Monica Burns and Barbara Ramirez. They are awesome. We have wonderful relationships with them.

"I need you to increase my Dilaudid. I can't handle the coughing, and the pain," Debbie says to Monica. "We can't figure out the proper number of additional pain pills. It changes every day. What works one day does not work the next."

A dark look comes over Monica's face.

"Debbie, you are already receiving a great deal of pain medication. If you are in this much pain...if I do this, you might not make it to Christmas. You want to be around for Christmas, don't you?"

"No. I'm ready to go," she says with minimal emphasis.

The air is knocked out of me. I can't breathe.

"I don't want to be here, anymore. This is not life. This is not living," Debbie continues.

The thought of Debbie not being around for Christmas is more than I can bear. Placing such a timeframe on the situation makes it far too real. Monica turns and stares at me without blinking. Her face is frozen blank. I realize she is struggling to confine and tamp down the emotions screaming inside her. She is very fond of Debbie. A tear makes its way out. She wipes it quick.

"Debbie, I don't let myself get close to my patients for this reason."

She hugs Debbie tight, and the tears flow.

"Promise me you will not let me suffer. I'm not afraid to die, I just don't want to be in pain."

"We will take very good care of you. You will pass peacefully."

Debbie rallied on Tuesday to oversee pie baking by the daughters-in-law and granddaughters. Wednesday, she did not get out of bed. Thursday, Thanksgiving Day, she was happy and alert all day, and well into the evening. She ate well, drank wine, posed for numerous pictures. It was a wonderful day. Since then, it has been a steep slide downhill.

Friday night, in the middle of the night, she awoke wanting to go to the bathroom. She could not stand at all so I carried her to the toilet. Later in the night, she tried to get out of bed on her own. I was able to stop her just before she fell. I am afraid to sleep.

It's now 10:22 a.m. on Tuesday, December 2nd, and I'm sitting bedside while Debbie sleeps. She makes terrible noises with her breathing, accentuated with wheezing, and moaning.

Night before last, after what I thought was a pretty good day, she told me, again, that she does not want to go on any longer; that what she is experiencing is not life; that she simply wants to go to sleep, and not wake up. She told me this while lucid, and with total sane clarity.

She also said, "I'm not leaving you, I love you, I just can't take any more. I have no strength left. I'm empty. Thank you for taking such good care of me. I know it's hard, but you have to let me go."

Actively letting her go, I am praying for God to take her sooner rather than later. She is suffering, so.

Yesterday, Monica increased Debbie's Dilaudid flow for what must be the fourth or fifth time since the pain pump was installed. She also told us the reason for Debbie's lack of urination—and when she does go about once per day, the terrible odor and odd color—is due to her one remaining kidney beginning to shut down.

Debbie expressed her desire to Monica to fall asleep and not wake up. Monica informed her, again, that as the Dilaudid flow rate continues to be increased, there will come a point when she will no longer care or even wake up. She will then, at some point, pass peacefully.

Monica also told me, alone, that as cancer patients lose interest in eating, their organs begin shutting down. The last to go are the heart, and lungs.

I must say I can only deal with the realities of this situation in an abstract sort of way. I simply do what I must do—doesn't matter what it is—while my thoughts try to catch up. I'll sort this all out, later.

How can I let go of my purpose for being and doing for over forty years? I can't solve that question while I am busy caring for what remains of the woman I love. I already see the ghost of her throughout our house in the things she has done, and in what we have done together. Aspects of her are apparent in our sons and granddaughters.

The truth is, I have been in a form of mourning for her since she discovered that first breast cancer over twenty-eight years ago. I pray I survive losing her. I pray my mourning will be replaced at some point with joy and hope at the thought of her. I found faith and love on a level few experience because of this excruciating process that has been our life. For that, I am eternally grateful.

After putting Debbie to bed this evening, I started watching a movie, *Up in the Air*, with George Clooney. I very much like the movie. In one part, a character reads from *Velveteen Rabbit*. I started crying, thinking of Debbie as my Velveteen Rabbit. Then, I had a vision of shelves lined with books. I thought of the stories of lives lived, lives lost, the good, the bad, the tragic, the heroic...

Debbie spoke with her cousin Lorraine a few days ago, and agreed to let her come for a farewell visit. I had been telling Lorraine no as instructed. Lorraine is in the midst of her own battle with cancer, and we're praying she wins.

Debbie and I are sitting in the family room on the couch. She seems in good spirits as she speaks with her sister on the phone. The doorbell rings. It is Lorraine and her husband Gerhard. I bring them into the family room. Lorraine sits on the couch next to Debbie, and hugs her.

"I am so happy to see you, sweetie," she says to Debbie.

"Hi, Lorraine," Debbie says.

Debbie's reaction to Lorraine's arrival is not as enthusiastic as I expected. She is looking at the floor. There is no smile, no questions for Lorraine; no funny comments for Gerhard. Earlier this morning she was looking forward to seeing Lorraine, but now I'm not seeing her usual rally when company arrives. Something has happened within her. There's no wind in her sails. She has reached empty, hit the wall, there's nothing left.

"Chuck, thank you so much for letting us come. I would have gone crazy if I did not get to see my dear cousin one last time. We are more like sisters than cousins. I know we will see each other soon on the other side. There is very little left for the doctors to do for my cancer. Debbie has been such an inspiration to me in my battle. I would have given up long ago if she had not kept after me to keep fighting."

Debbie raises her eyes, looks at me, and says, "I'm tired. I want to go into the bedroom. I want to go to bed."

# CHAPTER 15

# THE ROAD HOME

### *(Chuck)*

I'm numb. Pretty sure I can stay awake for the duration; forever, if need be. My senses and muscles are locked in readiness. I'm on a hair-trigger to love, and serve, and experience every last drop of Debbie.

Debbie is transitioning through a major decline that will leave her in a comatose state. She is beginning her fourth day with no food intake; second day without fluids. I swab her mouth and tongue every thirty minutes to keep them moist. She has lost the ability to swallow. Her one remaining kidney is shutting down along with the rest of her organs.

According to our hospice nurse, her relative youth makes the dying process much harder. As a result, she is experiencing strong "terminal restlessness." That is, she is trapped in a pattern of behavior she repeats incessantly. In her case, it began about thirty hours ago, with her getting in and out of bed saying, "I have to go to the bathroom." There is little comprehension on her part when attempting to reason with her. When assistance is offered, she climbs back into bed.

At one point, when Lorraine and I were with Debbie, we helped Debbie into the recliner next to our bed. She looked at us strangely.

"Debbie, do you know who we are?" I asked.

When she shook her head, and said no, I nearly fell down. It was as if my heart had been stomped on.

The constant getting in and out of bed is accelerating the pace of her weakening. She has lost most of her ability to speak. Our bed is one of those high pillow top things. She is unstable so I must be vigilant, as I do not want her to fall again. She gets very agitated if I try to take her to the bathroom. She was adamant about not wanting a hospital bed, but I requested one be delivered today. Going against her wishes bothers me a good deal, but her safety requires it. The bed rail will keep her from getting out of bed and falling. The thought of moving her out of the bed we have shared for so many years weighs heavy.

Lorraine and Gerhard come into the bedroom as I am helping Debbie into our bed again. Debbie pulls her nightgown up to her neck, exposing her naked self to all in the room. I try to cover her with the sheet, but she refuses. She looks at Lorraine and Gerhard with an I-don't-care-who-sees-me-naked, I'm-flipping-dying-here attitude. Gerhard is unfazed. He has that European attitude toward nudity. They sit down next to the bed.

"Ahh hod," she breathes.

"She's hot," I interpret, and decide not to care about her nakedness either.

Standing next to her, I look for a moment at the roadmap of scars covering her belly. Scars with stories, memories. Scars tracing a history of battle lines drawn with scalpels and stitches. Scars recording the infections that took months of wound care to achieve healing; the insertion points of various chest tubes, orthoscopic instruments, drainage lines, biopsy, and radio-frequency ablation probes. Scars upon scars where surgeons revisited her liver, and various other organs so many times, pulling her guts out for ease of close examination to remove tumors, and reroute plumbing.

Her body is the most beautiful testament to resilience, and never giving up, which I have ever beheld. I look at the reconstructed breasts she wanted so bad she subjected herself to an incredibly difficult surgery.

Breasts with tattooed nipples, rebuilt from her own fat tissue so as to avoid rejection by her body, and other issues implants had caused. The breast reconstruction that resulted in terrible infection in her lower belly at the site of the body-fat harvest. The infection that resulted in my gaining huge experience in wound care. Experience I put to good use battling post-operative infection a few more times. She was very prone to infection. I know more than most medical professionals about wound care. I learned life lessons in persistence and patience; to be okay with little improvements over weeks, months, and at times with major setbacks. Setbacks that knocked us on our asses, taking us down several rungs, back to the drawing board, countless steps in the wrong direction. We learned not to lose heart, but to stay with the problem, get up, and remain in the ring until that round in hell was only a scar.

"Don't worry about it," Lorraine offers. "Debbie never did mind too much that people saw her naked. Remember those beaches you guys went to? I was always the modest one. She always loved to shock me. I still have not gotten over seeing my father naked before he passed. We had to help take care of him. I thought the nurses should have done all those intimate things. I wish I had not been so insecure. I was so trapped in being prim and proper. Debbie was always so brave. I was always so jealous of her for that."

I turn the ceiling fan up a notch.

"I'll get more air moving. Maybe that will help," I say.

Interesting that Lorraine describes herself as being trapped. Makes sense—I feel bad for her. Debbie enjoyed life so much. Lorraine being jealous of Debbie for her fun approach to life is funny. Debbie was always jealous of Lorraine for her material wealth. Lorraine and Debbie were always at odds, competing with, and jealous of, each other. At the same time, they were completely devoted—sister-like in their relationship.

"I need to ask you something, and hope it don't upset you," Lorraine begins. "There are some old school books on your shelves upstairs that belonged to my grandparents when they were in grade school. If it is okay, I would like to take them with me; place them in the family archives."

Lorraine is the Pruden Family Historian; a self-appointed role she takes seriously. I attempt again to cover Debbie with a sheet. This time she does not object.

"Lorraine, I don't recall knowing anything about those books. You are welcome to them," I say.

"I hope you don't mind me asking this. I just think these books belong in the family archives."

"That's fine. If you know where they are, take them. I have no idea."

"There is something else, I don't want to discuss it right now, but at some point, I want to talk to you about Grandma Pruden's hope chest. That was passed to her by her mother, and...well, I don't want to talk about that right now, but that should probably also be placed in the family archives."

"You're right, we should talk about that another time, Lorraine."

She must perceive a dark look coming over my face as she drops the subject.

Debbie climbs out of bed. Her voice is barely intelligible.

"Baa...woom."

Thinking that if she used the toilet, this crazy cycle might end, I try to guide her toward the bathroom. She becomes agitated and scared. Now I know better and help her back into bed. What is going on in her mind? My heart breaks to watch her wear herself out in such an awful manner.

Brian, our oldest son, is on the other side of the planet. He is flying a C-40 mission, and should be back home within a few days. He did not want to be away right now, and asked his mom before leaving last week whether he should put in for emergency leave.

"I never want to stand in the way of you doing your job," she insisted. "If we had put life on hold every time I had a health problem over the years, we would not have accomplished a damn thing in our lives."

Her wisdom was beyond argument. Living up to the strong work ethic and sense of purpose she epitomizes, a tremendous point of pride for her, he left. Besides, at that point, the imminence of her passing was not so obvious.

Greg, Jen, and Addison are with Debbie so I can drive to Norfolk airport and pick up Nancy. I need time to chat with her before we get back to the house. It is going to be tough for Nancy to see her sister this way.

"How's our girl?" Nancy asks as we drive away from the terminal.

"Nancy, your sister is not well, at all. We are headed off the cliff. She is out of it most of the time due to the pain medications. With effort, you can bring her around. She might acknowledge you. She might not."

"What is Monica saying?" she asks, wanting the professional take.

"She says Debbie won't make it to the weekend," I answer.

We are silent for a bit.

"Debbie did not want you to have to come back," I say. "You were here just a few weeks ago. She wanted that to be your last memory of her...when she was still able to laugh, not gasping for her last breath."

"Yeah, well, she did not get a vote on this."

"I hear you. She gave lots of directions I have had to modify. She is not going through it from our perspective. I think she talked a good game about not wanting to be a bother, but she likes for people to go the extra mile for her."

"Nailed it! That's my sister."

"I'm really glad you are here. I want you to be prepared. She is not the person you remember. She did not recognize either Lorraine or me yesterday morning. She is wearing herself out with terminal restlessness. She is slowing down, but constantly getting in and out of bed. She can barely speak, anymore."

"Doesn't matter. I would be here no matter what."

"One thing I'm going against orders on: I ordered a hospital bed. It will be delivered later today. I can't put in another night with her climbing in and out of bed. I'm so afraid she is going to fall, again. Remember the fall she took out of bed at your house just before we were going to Disney World?" I ask.

"Yeah, that was scary. You have to do what you have to do. Have you been able to get any sleep?" she asks.

"Not much. Couldn't sleep if I tried. I'm pretty wired."

"You have to get some rest. Your family needs you to be there when the shit hits the fan."

"I'm fine. I'll be there. My biggest concern is Debbie will pass on Addison's birthday."

"That would be just like my sister. She wants to make sure her grand-daughters remember her."

Being Sunday, there is little traffic. We arrive at my house after a twenty-minute drive. Nancy goes directly to the bedroom. Greg and Jen are there bedside, and stand as Nancy arrives.

"Hi, Aunt Nancy."

"Hi, you two. How are you holding up?"

She is focused on Debbie as she gives quick hugs to Greg and Jen.

"Debbie, it's me, your favorite sister. Debbie, can you hear me? I'm here."

Debbie labors to open her eyes. A look of recognition is on her face. She makes unintelligible sounds. She seems to put all her strength into looking at Nancy's face for a short span. Her attention fades. She closes her eyes.

"I love you, sis," Nancy whispers into Debbie's ear as she hugs her.

"Aunt Nancy," an excited Addison squeals as she enters the room. "It's my birthday in four more days!"

"Really? How old are you going to be?"

"Five years old."

"Oh my goodness, I can't believe it," Nancy says as she gets a quick hug from Addison.

Addison climbs on the bed, and gives her Mimi a hug.

"I love you, Mimi!"

Debbie responds by opening her eyes, and producing the closest thing to a smile I have seen since Thanksgiving, nine days in the past.

"Ah uh ooh," she says.

"I love you," Nancy interprets, a quick study. She turns to me with a startled look on her face, and whispers, "I'm going to call my brothers, and tell them if they want to see their sister again, they need to get on the road right away."

She leaves the room, and returns after about ten minutes.

"They're all coming," she informs me. "Debbie, your brothers are on their way to see you. Do you hear me? Bob, Gary, and Rick are driving down to see you. Bob and Rick are driving to Gary's tonight. They are driving here together in the morning."

Debbie opens her eyes for a moment, but it is unclear that she understands what Nancy is saying.

"Where is Brian?" Nancy asks me.

"He is making his way from the western Pacific. Should arrive in Hawaii later today, then fly the rest of the way home, with a brief stop in San Diego, arriving sometime tomorrow night."

Nancy expresses her concern by means of a worried look in my direction, and a glance in Debbie's direction.

"Debbie insisted he go on this mission," I say.

"I know, she told me."

"He will be back in time," I assure her.

"I hope so," she replies.

The hours of the day pass. Nancy remains bedside with me. Debbie climbs out of bed countless times. Others come and go. Our minister stops by. I bring him up to speed on Debbie's condition. We pray together. He departs.

Monica stops by late in the afternoon.

"This agitated behavior she is experiencing has to stop," she says, shaking her head with pity and concern. "Chuck, you need some rest.

Let other people help you. I'm increasing her Dilaudid flowrate, again. She should rest much better tonight."

The doorbell rings a bit after 9:00 p.m. It's the hospice medical equipment guy delivering the hospital bed. He and I are quite familiar with each other after so many deliveries and discussions.

"Was beginning to think you were not going to make it today," I say.

"It's been a busy day. I've been all over Hampton Roads. How is your wife doing?"

"Not well. I need that bed pretty bad."

I help him bring the pieces of the bed into the foyer from his truck. "I have a spot in the bedroom all ready for it," I say.

We carry the pieces into the bedroom where Nancy is holding her sister's hand. I feel terrible about doing this, setting up this hospital bed for Debbie. She specifically said she does not want to die in a hospital bed. Why am I doing this? I must justify anything I do in variance from Debbie's stated wishes or I know I will beat myself up for it. I may do that, anyway. That would be like me to do.

A small part of me worries her passing in our bed will haunt me. I focus on my concerns about her falling from our high mattress. I have been unable to sleep because I have no way of preventing her from falling without constant vigilance. Hospital beds have safety-rails for this very reason. I also worry about her ruining our mattress. Not because I am too cheap to buy a new one, but because I know I will take great comfort in sleeping where Debbie and I enjoyed so much time together: memories of holding each other, talking, making love...

Debbie is totally out of it. She is taking no notice of what I am doing. The increased flow of pain medication has her resting well, now. We finish assembling the bed. The equipment guy opens a box with an air mattress that inflates and deflates various chambers, in a sequence that is helpful in preventing bedsores. We open plastic bags containing bedsheets, and finish our work. I walk him out.

I return to the bedroom, and sit down next to Nancy.

"She has not moved for a few hours. I think Monica got her under control," Nancy observes.

"I think so, too. I hate that she is so out of it, though. Debbie did not want to experience any pain, but she also wanted to be clearheaded, and able to communicate at the end. That's a tough set of desires to accomplish together."

"She always sets the bar high," Nancy says, and smiles.

"That's for sure. She is resting well. I need for her to sleep in our bed with me one more night," I say, and Nancy tears up looking at me.

"Are you sure? You need rest."

"I'll move her tomorrow. I want one more night with her next to me. She's down for the night. Don't think she's going to move a bit."

An hour later, Nancy goes to bed. I climb in next to Debbie, and cuddle up to her. Oh my god, her body is bone-hard, stiff as a corpse. This is awful. Not what I was wanting as a last memory in bed with her. I don't sense any presence of my wife. I talk to her, hoping somehow the person I love is hearing me, knows I am here.

"I love you, Debbie. I love you with everything I've got. I'm going to miss you so much. This sucks."

I let the statement hang out there, somewhere in the universe, waiting, waiting for a reply.

"Big time," I say, completing our duet myself.

Somehow, I fall asleep, but movement brings me back, ready for action. Debbie has gotten out of bed. In a flash, I get out of my side of the bed, and sprint around to her, afraid she is about to fall. She is standing next to the bed, holding on.

"Honey! Hang on, I'm here, baby."

With my hand on her back, I reach over, and bring up additional light. The hospital bed looms in the far end of the room. It's time; it's what I must do. Face-to-face in front of her, I hold her close for what I know is our last real hug. There is no reaction, no embrace from her in return. Stepping back from her, she looks dazed and confused as I take her hands in my own.

"I need you to come with me, baby."

Facing her, holding her hands in mine like we are at a kindergarten dance, I walk backward, aiming toward the hospital bed. Dear god, this is awful. Wish I didn't have to do this. With tiny stiff-legged steps, she is following my lead; trusting me, from somewhere in her mind, when I feel least worthy.

The bed she railed against is where I am taking her.

I hate this moment.

I hate myself.

Frankenstein's walking style flashes through my mind as we shuffle along. The thought makes me angry. Can't bear to think of Debbie as Frankenstein. Fighting through the thought, I continue to lead the hideous march across a dance floor of horrors. Dancing, I wish we were dancing at a wedding right now. Dear God, help me. We make it to her new bed, and she lies down without any fuss. Wow, that makes me feel better. Thought for sure she would object, fight me.

Covering her with a sheet and thin blanket, I realize she will not be rising from there, alive. Lifting the safety-rail, a sense of great relief clicks into place. She is safe now. No more falls. Moving my black recliner from the corner of the room, I position it snug up next to her. Reclining alongside her, outside the safety-rail, I take her hand in mine.

"Thank you, God," I say, out loud. "Does this look like another piece of the puzzle, from on high?" I ask Debbie.

It isn't long before she tries climbing through the safety-rail. Well, this isn't going to work. What can I do? I notice leftover scrap sections of foam-filled poster board. The granddaughters have made wonderful works of art on them with magic markers. Perfect! Using wide box tape, I secure a few pieces in place on the inside of the safety-rail to prevent Debbie's legs from coming through. She continues to try to escape, but my contraption is working. Reclining, I again reach through the rail for Debbie's hand.

Sam Smith is singing in my head about not crying when she's gone, lying next to her, taking care of her...I cry, then doze.

Nancy's mouth drops open in surprise when she walks into the bedroom at 6:00 a.m. Still holding Debbie's hand, I am awake.

"I wasn't expecting to see my sister in that bed."

"I couldn't believe it. She got out of bed in the night; had to move her. I steadied her, and she walked over here on her own, and got into bed without any fuss. Hated doing it, but this is much safer."

"What's with the fancy poster board taped to the rail?"

"She was trying to climb through the rail. That keeps her feet and legs from coming through. Would you like to sit here with your sister while I make us some coffee?"

"About time I got some service around here. Was expecting coffee delivered to me in bed. You used to do that for Debbie, why not me?"

"Sorry, I'm getting pretty lax in my duties."

Bringing the recliner into an upright position, I get to my feet. Nancy takes over my position holding Debbie's hand.

"Good morning, my sister."

Nancy works to bring Debbie to consciousness, and continues her soothing talk as I step into the bathroom to brush my teeth, and make my way to the kitchen.

Monica arrives a bit after 9:00 a.m.

"I'm glad to see you got her into the hospital bed. It makes it much easier to care for her."

Monica checks Debbie's temperature, pulse, blood pressure.

"She is declining faster than I expected. Her vitals all indicate her situation is imminent. She's within forty-eight hours of passing," Monica informs us. "How are you doing?"

"I'm okay," I respond.

"Have you had any sleep?"

"I've had a few bits, and pieces. I can't turn my brain off. Debbie needs me constantly, and I don't want to miss out on any time with her."

"You must let other people help you. Take something to help you sleep. Go upstairs where it's quiet, and let yourself rest for a few hours. If you don't, you are going to fall down when you're needed most."

"My brothers will be here in a few hours. Between us, we can take care of Debbie," offers Nancy.

"I hate taking things to help me sleep. Sleeping pills give me weird dreams, and leave me groggy."

"Take a Valium. It will relax you, allow you sleep for a few hours, and wear off quick—very little grogginess."

"Okay, okay, I'll do it."

"When does your son get back?" Monica asks.

"He should be here tonight. I hope Debbie will recognize him."

"Either Barbara or I will stop by later today. Call me anytime, day or night."

"Thank you, Monica."

"Yes, thank you, Monica. You and Barbara have been wonderful to my sister. She tells me every time I talk to her how happy she is with your care of her."

"Yes, well we both think the world of Debbie. I try to not get so close to my patients, but couldn't help it with her. She is very special, and way too young for this to be happening."

Monica departs.

Debbie's brothers arrive around noon. Returning the recliner to the far corner of the room, I bring a variety of other chairs into position alongside the bed. Arranging deck chairs on the Titanic comes to mind. Nancy helps her brothers wake Debbie enough to acknowledge her kin. She opens her eyes, and makes weak sounds, communicating with each brother. She fades back out. They are shocked by what they see.

"Nancy warned us about her condition, but I was not prepared to see her this way," says the oldest brother, Bob.

"She was doing so well when MaryAnn and I were here a few weeks ago with the kids, and those pictures she posted on Facebook from

Thanksgiving—she looked so great. She was goofing around, having fun, making faces..." observes Gary, the youngest brother.

"I really thought she would beat this thing, again. Just like she always has," says Rick. "There has to be something they can do for her?"

Rick is a few years older than Debbie, and one year younger than Bob.

"I'll give you folks time with Debbie while I take a nap. I'm under strict orders to take drugs, and get some rest before I fall down. Gotta be awake when Brian gets here tonight."

Upstairs, in one of the guest rooms, the drug takes me to strange dreams. Awaking with a start, hating the feeling of paranoia, I have been asleep for about three hours. Dizzy and disoriented, I get to my feet, and return downstairs to my bedroom. It is filled with chairs holding loved ones. Laughter breaks out as old stories are told one after another. Pizza is ordered, delivered, and consumed.

At 10:00 p.m., Brian calls. He has landed, and will drive directly to our house. He arrives less than an hour later. I am so happy to see him. We are complete now. He hugs his way into the room until he is standing next to his mom, bends down over her, holds her...

"I'm here, Mama. I love you," he says. "It's Brian. Your favorite son."

Sure am glad I have a large bedroom as it has taken on the form of an arena with concentric rows of seating aimed at the star on center stage. Sort of a mini-theatre for a small stage production. Barley, Greg and Jen's golden retriever, works the crowd for pats on the head. Brian answers plenty of questions regarding his Navy career, and most recent flight mission. Memories are shared as they rise to the surface of minds present. Laughs come easy. The vigil force remains strong through the night. A few decide to catch a brief sleep upstairs or on one of the couches. "Wake me in an hour," is the norm.

Brian does not leave the room. He climbs into our bed, and shuts his eyes, but I sense he is not going to sleep. Nancy and I take turns holding Debbie's hand, and swabbing her mouth to keep it from getting too dry. The button providing additional injections of Dilaudid is liberally pushed whenever Debbie moans with pain. We catch tiny snatches of sleep reclining on my chair in the corner.

Sunrise brings everyone back into the bedroom. It's Tuesday. I wish I could stop time's flow. The aroma of coffee and bagels is strong. Addison is in a state of constant excitement having so many family members here.

Erin arrives midmorning with fresh clothes for Brian. Their daughters Aubrey and Layla are with her. They each hug Debbie, and get varying degrees of response from her. Like a coral reef, the room is in a constant state of flow with life-sustaining currents crossing over, under, and through each other. Somewhere in her mind, Debbie must be enjoying our presence. This is exactly what she envisioned for her deathbed scene except she wanted to be more interactive.

Waves of food continue to wash ashore on my kitchen counters. It's as if I am walking a beach finding what the tide has brought in: casseroles, KFC, cakes, donuts...

In the early afternoon, Erin announces she must get the girls home for naps, or they will be miserable later. She hugs Debbie goodbye, gathers the girls under protest, and departs. About ten minutes later, Aubrey runs headlong into the bedroom directly to Debbie, and pounces on her with a big hug.

"Bye bye, Mimi, I love you," she says, and squeezes her grandmother tight with her little arms.

Debbie becomes the most alert she has been for a few days. She returns Aubrey's hug, and as their eyes connect in a forever moment, Debbie says, "Aah uhh oooo, uhway."

"Mimi said she loves you, Aubrey," Brian interprets.

The scene scorches a place in my memory I will always be able to return to. Aubrey gives Debbie a kiss, and as quick as she came in, turns, and runs out of the room. Erin, with tears in her eyes, explains what happened.

"We were driving home. Just as I was passing you guys' church, I hear Aubrey saying from the backseat, 'Mommy, I didn't hug Mimi goodbye!' Something about her little voice made me do a U-turn right there, and bring her back."

"I'm so glad you did," says Brian. "That was one of the most amazing things I have ever witnessed. It was beautiful. Aubrey loves her Mimi."

"Thank you so much, Erin, for bringing her back," I say. "Whatever possessed you to do that?"

"I don't know. I just knew I had to come back."

Erin departs, again.

It's about 2:30 p.m., and I'm in the kitchen when I hear commotion emanating from the bedroom.

"Chuck, Debbie's awake. Come quick!"

I sprint. Debbie is wide awake. The upper part of the bed has been raised to support her seeing everyone. She is fully alert, looking around the room at all of us gathered there, and trying to speak.

"Ah uh ooo."

Other sounds she makes are impossible to understand. We all know she is telling us goodbye. She raises her arms to us. We take turns receiving hugs. Her face is radiant. I've never seen her more perfect, more beautiful. All of us talk to her at once, a chorus of loved ones: her sister, her brothers, her two sons, one daughter-in-law, Jen, and myself.

For half an hour, we continue to tell her how much we love her, and feel that love returned. Addison is with us.

"It's okay for you to go, sis."

"It's okay, Mom, we'll be okay."

"It's okay, honey. I'll be okay, I promise. We'll all be okay. I love you, so much. We had a hell of a ride, baby."

We all grow silent as she looks deep into each of us with a slight smile that lights up the depths of our souls. Without warning, it's as if a switch is flipped off. I feel dizzy as if the earth has gone out of focus beneath me. It is obvious that Debbie's soul, her essence, has left the building. Debbie's face has gone dark. Time passes. I'm adrift, out of contact with reality. Somewhere, Barley is barking, barking, barking; bringing me back to the spot where I am frozen in place. She must be outside barking at a squirrel or a neighbor dog. Barking, barking, barking.

"What's with Barley?" I ask Greg.

Greg leaves the room. Conversation returns to the room.

"What just happened?"

"She just slipped into a coma."

"That was the most amazing thing I have ever seen."

"She looked like an angel. There was light coming from inside her."

"I could hear her talking in my head."

"I've heard and read about this sort of thing happening. They call it 'Holding Court.' People suddenly become fully alert on their deathbed, and have time for final farewells."

Greg returns to the room. Barley is still barking.

"I closed Barley in our bedroom this morning. She never barks when she is in there. She just lays on the bed, and chills. I walked into the room just now, and she was barking at the ceiling in the corner of the room. I tried to get her to stop, but she just kept barking. I decided to just close the door and leave."

Barley stops barking.

"Debbie has left the building."

Debbie is now in a coma. No moans, no response whatsoever from attempts to bring her around. Our vigil settles in for the long haul. Monica visits, and confirms Debbie is in a coma state. She says she has witnessed and heard stories about several other "Holding Court" occurrences.

"She is likely to pass within twenty-four hours. It's hard to say for sure. She is young, and her heart is strong. That will make her passing harder, but I think it will be soon."

As much as I hate to think it, I hope she passes before Addison's birthday.

190

Everyone is hovering nearby: Brian, Nancy, Greg, and Jen. It's the middle of the night, early Thursday morning. Debbie's brothers left sometime yesterday afternoon—can't recall when. We take turns holding her hand, seated in one of the chairs tight up to her hospital bed. I could remove the sections of foam poster board I taped in place to keep her legs in the bed when she was going through the compulsive movement, but I don't.

I place my hand on her chest. Her heart has been racing, pounding so hard for hours. Her breathing is a combination of labored rasping, and rattling wheezes. Debbie is gone. How long can her body continue to do this? Connected, my breathing matches hers. During long pauses I hold my own, inhaling only when her tumor-filled lungs pull in more air. I am connected to her. How can I let her go? I take her hand.

"We had one hell of a ride, baby. I love you. It's okay. You can go now. I will see you in heaven. Say hi to everyone for me."

Dear God, please give Debbie's body rest. I know she is already with you. I love her so. Thank you for sharing her with me.

Her breathing stops. Her heart continues its rapid drumroll. How can it not come jumping out of her chest? I keep holding my breath. Her heart stops, then one, two more strong throbs.

That's it? How is this possible? She's gone.

My wife is dead. This can't be real. How can there be a world without her? My breath comes roaring back into my chest, and I start to sob, loud. Tears pour down my face. Those standing close to me are also sobbing, wailing. I kiss and hug my wife's body. We take turns hugging her. I look at the clock on the television remote box, and subtract a few minutes to deduce her passing occurred at 5:11 a.m.

Numb, I call Monica. She will call the undertaker, and come over right away. Time is coming at me in a way I have never experienced before. My mind is in a place I have never been before. Monica and Barbara arrive, and Nancy and I stand nearby as they prepare Debbie's body for transport. Monica brushes Debbie's hair. They remove her

191

nighty, and adult diaper. Rolling her from side to side, they wash her stiff body.

"Is there a favorite pretty dress you would like to dress her in?" asks Monica.

"I don't know, she has lots of nice dresses," I hear myself say from somewhere.

"We'll find something," Erin says.

She and Jen go into our large walk-in closet to make a selection. I stand looking at Debbie's naked body, transfixed. Jen and Erin ask me to decide between some things. We decide on black slacks, white blouse, and a pink sweater.

"Pink was always her favorite color," I say, hoping Debbie would approve.

The nurses dress Debbie with great efficiency, and position her like Sleeping Beauty with her head on the pillow, and arms at her side. Nancy also brushes her sister's hair. Debbie would want to look as well as possible.

"The men coming to pick her up should be here soon. You should give everyone alone time to say goodbye to her," Monica advises.

"Okay," I say.

"I'll go first. I'll come out when I am done, and whoever is next can come in," Nancy says, and remains.

I leave the room, and organize the others. Everything I say and do is happening on automatic pilot.

Nancy comes out with tears tracking down her face. Brian and Erin go in, holding each other together. Then Greg and Jen. The couples cannot hug or be hugged too tight. I go in last. I kiss her forehead. Hard as marble. I hold her hand. Stiff and cold. Place my hand on her chest. It is empty. Floating above my body, I'm in some form of shock.

"They're here," Nancy says, entering the room.

"I loved her with everything I had," I say.

"I know you did, and she loved you the same way. You were the best husband to her anyone could ask for. Now, you must be okay without her. You promised."

"I was lying," I say.

"Well, I'm going to hold you to it," Nancy says.

Monica comes into the room.

"I recommend you all go upstairs. Don't be down here when they take her out. You do not want that to be your final memory of her," Monica says from obvious experience.

The thought of missing any possible second with her is hard to take, but I concede to Monica.

"Okay, I'll be right out."

Monica and Nancy depart.

"Goodbye, baby, I already miss you so much. You are in a much better place now, but I wish you were here with me. I'm selfish, that way."

I touch her face, the face that has inspired me for forty years, give her a final kiss on her forehead, and walk out of the room with a brief stop for a last look.

In the foyer, I meet and shake hands with the men who will remove Debbie's body from our home. They are wearing dark suits, and ties, at 7:00 a.m.

"Take good care of her, guys," I say.

"The very best, Mr. Wilson. We are sorry for your loss."

Upstairs, I hang out in Debbie's sewing room with Brian. Monica comes to get us.

"She's gone. They did a great job with her. Barbara and I are leaving now."

I give her a hug.

"Thank you so much, Monica. I could not have done this without you."

I make it downstairs, and give Barbara a hug, and thanks. They are wonderful, beautiful women.

"We had to collect all of the prescription narcotics Debbie had left."

"Ah, good," I say, glad to have those out of the house.

They depart, and I instinctively walk into the bedroom. There, the hospital bed is neatly made with Debbie's favorite (mauve?) blanket as a bed cover. Her mother knitted that for her. A silk rose is on the pillow. The thoughtful and beautiful sight brings tears to my eyes. I have everyone come and look at it.

I am so glad Debbie passed so early this morning, and that she was taken out of the house before Addison woke up. Sitting in my bedroom in the black leather recliner, I am reading the many wonderful postings coming in from friends and family. My mind is traveling through time, crossing the span of my life with Debbie. Addison hops into the room—can't help but smile. She climbs up on my lap.

"Papa, I know my Mimi died today. Inside I have a sad face for Mimi, but on the outside, I'm smiling and bouncing because it's my birthday. I'm five!"

# CHAPTER 16

# A MIGHTY FORCE

### *(Chuck)*

I had always assumed I knew what it meant to take life one day at a time. We faced enough challenges to get this concept. Well, the two days since Debbie's passing have been protracted like one of those house of mirrors rooms with reverse reflections that stretch to infinity. First, I can't believe it has only been two days. My sense of time is totally distorted. It's hard to put things that have happened in their proper place in time: Did that happen this morning? Yesterday morning? Last night? So much has happened this past week, and I do not want any of it to slip from memory—even the painful moments.

The shock that held me together through the first day is wearing off. I spent last night second-guessing Debbie's decisions, and concessions I made to support her decisions. I finally declared a truce with myself this morning. The truth is, Debbie ran out of ammunition long ago, but kept on fighting because she knew I could not bear to let her go. She had to *make* me allow her to go. That was the hardest concession of them all. I was (am) addicted to her, and the withdrawal process is excruciating.

The letting go process is sometimes abruptly accelerated by the arrival of things, like Debbie's obituary which ran in our local paper, as well as the papers in our hometowns of Corning and Elmira, New York.

195

*Debra Lee Wilson, 58, of Chesapeake, passed away following a twenty-eight-year battle with cancer on Thursday, December 11, 2014.*

*Daughter of the late Donald, and Shirley Pruden, originally of Campbell, NY, Debbie attended high school in Bath, NY. She, and her husband began dating when they were both age seventeen, and married a few years later. She resided in several states as her husband, a career naval officer, was transferred around the country. She achieved a Masters degree in Education, and worked as an elementary school teacher. She loved to travel, meet people, and spend time with her family or at her favorite hobbies of quilting, knitting, and other crafts. Her indomitable spirit inspired many, especially her fellow cancer warriors, and she maintained wonderful relationships with friends all over the world.*

*Survivors include her devoted husband of thirty-seven years, Charles Wilson, Jr.; sons, Brian (Erin), and Gregory Wilson (Jennifer); granddaughters, Addison, Aubrey, and Layla; siblings, Robert Pruden (Yolanda), Rick Pruden, Gary Pruden (MaryAnn), and Nancy Pruden Keefer (Chris); stepmother, Harriet Pruden. She also leaves behind a large extended family, and countless special friends.*

I am feeling a strong and strange urge to get away, to return *home*, to be where she wants her remains to rest. Returning home evokes a powerful full-circle feeling. The church is within arrow shot of her home while growing up in Bath, as well as the middle and high schools she attended. Just a few doors down, you can still buy her favorite English Cuts (local doughnut) at the decades-old downtown bakery.

As the days dwindle on, I feel anchor-less, adrift, a bit confused. I kept thinking over and over about something Debbie and I said to each other, somewhat humorously, several times as the end approached: "This sucks!" one of us would say. The other would respond, "Big time!" I have many friends offering to be someone for me to talk to, but I only want to talk to Debbie, and often do. It feels natural—not crazy—I hope.

I still don't get it. I don't understand how it is that she is not, and cannot, be here in earthly, touchable, hold-able form. At my very basic self, I need her so much to be here I am screaming inside. If I were alone in the house, I would really be letting it rip, yelling at God and the universe to bring her back to me, but I refrain. I don't want to frighten my granddaughter, Addison, or my son Greg, or daughter-in-law Jen. I am so thankful for them to be living in the house with me.

I've been married since I was twenty years old. I am so used to being in a relationship with someone I love—to the *core*—that it is hard to relate to people in their thirties or forties who have never married or had children. I feel sorry for my nephews who are still wandering the earth without soulmates.

Yesterday afternoon I was lying down in our bed in absolute agony. First, Gary called to check on me. My grief was bubbling over as we talked. Then Nancy called. She spoke with such clarity, insight, and strength in a voice so like Debbie's that tears flowed from both eyes in steady streams down my face. With the release of the tears, I began to feel better. It was almost like being released from prison or finding my way out of a cave into the light.

The funeral home calls on Christmas Eve informing me Debbie's ashes are ready to be picked up. Having her remains with me for Christmas makes a part of me happy—hope that is not too deranged.

Sitting alone in my bedroom, I'm listening to music and thinking about Debbie. Her ashes are about ten feet away. This is my first New Year's Eve without a kiss from my beloved. It's hard to care about the start of a new year. I think of the Prayer Shawl Ministries Debbie started at our churches in both Covington, Tennessee and Bonita Springs, Florida. People have reached out to me over the past few days to tell me how important those initiatives have been to so many people: those who received as well as the ladies who made them. Together, there have been nearly two thousand prayer shawls presented to individuals going through challenging times. Imagining so many people wrapped in prayers makes me feel good.

Have been spending a lot of time in our bedroom where she passed. I set up something of a shrine to her on the spot where she died. Having her ashes, pictures, candles, rocking chair, afghan, nightgown she passed in, and the rose the hospice nurses left on her pillow brings me great comfort. I may be a bit crazy.

My intention is to depart for New York tomorrow, January 1st. Kris and Becky Goodrich have offered me their log home outside of Bath as a place to stay for a few weeks. They have moved to their new lake-house, but have not yet been able to sell their cabin. I have lots of organizing and packing to accomplish if I'm leaving tomorrow. While in New York, I'll work on some writing, reconnect with old friends from high school, and maybe organize a fortieth reunion.

If I can just remember to choose joy when I think of Debbie, I think I can avoid the pit of despair. Perhaps that is a lesson to be taken from her passing on Addison's birthday.

At Debbie's memorial service in Chesapeake, Addison was sitting next to me drawing on the back of a large white envelope. She had written "love" in large letters, and drawn matching stick figures on either side. On the left, the face of the stick figure had an oval mouth that was darkened in. On the right, the stick figure had a smiley face. Addison told me both stick figures were pictures of her. The one with the oval mouth was her on the inside, sad for Mimi. The other was her on the outside, happy. She chose joy! We can learn so much from children as to how we should live, and think as adults.

I feel the need to use this as a kind of jumping off point; a launchpad for something positive. I'm beginning to feel like a caged bull, raging against my confinements. I need to get out, roam, paw the earth, and get into adventures.

I want to set a new course—continue from where my travels with Debbie brought me. Whether I'm adrift or castaway on an island, I am alone right now, with only an inkling of a purpose. I *must* decide on, and be, someone I would admire and be proud of. Someone my children and grandchildren will hold in esteem, and strive to be or surpass. I need to set the bar high for them, and not be a disappointment to myself by focusing on the unfairness of the universe.

Greg, Jen, and Addison return home from a New Year's Eve party. Addison comes into my bedroom.

"I need to jump on your bed," she announces and proceeds to do so.

With waves of excited happiness beaming from her up and down face, the bedcovers pull and move until they resemble the ocean around a storm.

"Happy New Year!" I say to her.

"Everybody says that," she replies, a bit quizzical. "Every day is a new year, sometimes!"

Her statement somehow folds perfectly into what I was just thinking

---- CHAPTER 17 ----

# DIVERGENCE

*(Chuck)*

Awaking from a dream, Debbie's eyes are in my head. Sitting up on the edge of the bed, I think about what it means. It is a recurring dream I have had many versions of lately. This time, I dreamt I awoke from a dream into another dream. In the first dream, I was driving my car, loaded full of stuff, to a new job somewhere in the northeast. There was an important meeting, and I was running late. Troubles of all kinds conspired to keep me from getting there. When I get to a place where the road is closed due to construction, I drive around the barricades, and edge my way past huge holes in the highway. Getting to the meeting is imperative to me. My car gets hung up, and is teetering on a partially deconstructed bridge. Mangled rebar, twisted girders, and emptiness gape and sneer at me from below. I unstrap a mini-bike from the rear bumper, and negotiate my way along a narrow path that remains on the left side of the bridge. Arriving at a point where there is no bridge left, only emptiness ahead of me, I get frustrated.

"Dear God, why did you bring me here?" I scream.

Awaking from that dream into what I think is reality, I am so glad that what I was experiencing is not real. Realizing I fell asleep in my hammock, I breathe in the cool air, and consider the perfect blueness of the sky. My completion of some yard work before lying down, the

200

drudgery of bagging lots of leaves, replays in my head. My muscles are sore. This hammock was a Father's Day gift a few years ago, but I rarely ever use it myself—there is always too much to do. Debbie is rocking me, and while it is a reversal of our usual roles, it somehow seems perfectly normal that she should be.

"Thanks for covering me up with your mom's god-awful afghan," I say, noticing the gaudy, multicolored thing keeping me warm.

"I know it's ugly, but I love it. You looked like you might be getting cold," she says as I watch her face appear and disappear at the edge of my swinging hammock.

"Thank you, baby. You're so good to me," I say. "I had the craziest dream. I was trying to make my way to a big meeting, some new job in the northeast, possibly near Boston. Not sure. It ended with me on a bridge that was being torn down, and me screaming at God for bringing me there."

We laugh.

"Thank you for always making me laugh," she says. "I love you."

She continues to rock me. I love this moment, and the way her face bobs up and down, in and out of view.

"I love you, too," I respond. "It's a bit strange for you to be rocking me. I'm always the one who rocks you."

"Yes, you've always rocked me," she says with a heavy dose of sexual innuendo.

We laugh.

"Dreams can seem so real, and everything makes sense while you're dreaming, but then, when you wake up...you wonder how it is you did not know it was a dream."

"Yeah, it's funny," I say.

"Remember the story you have been working on for years about the pelican you rescued from between the ships in Long Beach?" she asks.

"Sure do. Someday I will figure it out, and it will be a great Christmas story. It will replace all other Christmas stories as everyone's favorite. It will make us rich and famous!" I say.

We both laugh. Each pendulum swing appearance of her brown eyes, and sparkling face, shines joy into my heart.

"You are the pelican. The task is your ladder," she says.

Confused, I think for a moment considering what she is saying.

"I thought you were the pelican," I respond.

"You have to let me go. The vow was *until death do us part*," she says, and a sweet smile comes slow to her face.

Reality hits me like a plank in the face as I awake with a start, and my heart breaks again. Debbie's eyes are in my head. Sitting up on the edge of the bed, I reconcile my mind with the reality Debbie has been dead for fifteen months.

She comes to me often in my dreams. Sometimes I know she is dead, and just on some sort of day trip from heaven—like the time I dreamed of picking her up at a bus stop. She was with a group of about sixty ladies coming down to visit loved ones. It was a jocular group of all sizes, and ages, wearing smiles, and excited to be visiting grieving sons, daughters, spouses, lovers...Debbie came off the bus as she was in her thirties—drop-dead gorgeous. We spent a few hours together, holding each other in a hotel bed. Returning her to the bus, the other ladies are arriving. Some are carrying shopping bags, some are wearing new hats.

"What have you two been up to?" someone cajoles.

Knowing laughter erupts. We both smirk.

"Sorry we didn't do any shopping," I say, recalling how much Debbie enjoys bargain hunting.

"I *shop* with my sister," she says. "I make *love* with you."

Her smile and twinkling eyes resonate through the chambers of my soul. Sounds of glee emanate from the bus, and arms wave as the happy ladies pull away. I love that dream.

However, the norm is I awake from dreams of Debbie unaware of her passing. The experience of disappointment, the hell of reality set-tling in, is the bitter cream-filling at the center of my breakfast-mourning doughnut.

I'm not dreaming now. Making my feet, I head to the bathroom. Flipping on the lights. The *me* in the mirror is much changed. My platinum hair, as I call it, is the longest it has been since before I went off to the Navy, thirty-five years ago. My month's growth of beard is also platinum. Comparisons to Hemingway make me feel better than being called Santa. I'm trying to be a writer, after all.

"You are the pelican," I repeat from my dream to the image in the mirror. "The task is your ladder."

I get it. I must let her go—diverge. The word diverge has come to mind again and again these past few days.

A special Christmas Eve, so many years ago, comes to mind. Brian and Greg, are spending the day onboard *Lewis B. Puller* with me. I am the ship's Chief Engineer, and it is my turn to serve as Command Duty Officer. With minimal crew onboard, little is going on. The pelican is trapped in a small space of open water between my ship and a sister-frigate, moored alongside. Two huge sea cushions, on either side of the pelican's little bit of water, seal him in like matching bookend-tombstones. There was enough space for the bird to land, probably dove on a fish, but not enough to take flight. The purpose of sea-cushions is to prevent ships from bumping, and grinding against each other while moored side-by-side.

Near death after three days without food, the winged fisherman will surely die without my assistance. The boys notice the bird while accompanying me on my rounds of the ship.

"Ah, that pelican has been there since we pulled into port the other day," I say. "Don't think he can get out."

"Can't we help him?" Brian asks.

"Yeah, Dad. We must help him. I love pelicans," says Greg.

"Not sure what I can do, boys," I respond. "Thought sure he would make his own way out."

Oh man, I have to do something now that the boys have seen that bird. Recruiting help from both ships, we tie ropes to a bucket, lower it between the ships and, as if animated by some great puppet-master, we try to scoop the pelican out. The pelican resists our efforts. Pinocchio's rebellion against the kindly Geppetto comes to mind.

What to do, what to do? Looking around, I notice a stokes litter mounted to the side of my ship next to a lifesaver ring. Stokes litters are stretchers used to carry injured sailors. Made of stainless steel tubing, and what appears to be chicken wire, there are straps to hold a hurt individual in place. Ropes at the four corners allow ambulation within, and around, the challenging environment of a ship.

It occurs to me that if we lowered the litter between the ships, and lean one end against a sea-cushion with the other end in the water, the pelican might make use of it as a ramp. It might understand, and be okay with a climb out of death, I think.

Bam! The story I have been struggling to understand for so long now applies to me. I need a method I can understand to climb out of the pit; to rejoin life for my remaining days on this planet. To diverge from my old self, and walk toward the next me. The new me. The task is the means to the end—to understand, and achieve perspective. The task is the writing of this story in a way that makes it readable, fun, interesting, life-changing, of help to anyone and everyone—especially those going through hell.

The pelican, I recall, waddles up the stokes litter, makes its way the length of the capsule-shaped sea cushion, and jumps into the water, accessing freedom on the other side. It then uses most of the available space to make the air, but with a steep rip-rapped seawall looming in its flightpath, it dives left, out of our sight.

"Stupid bird!" I say.

So, I'm the pelican, huh!

My task, my process of diverging, includes things I've already felt compelled to do. The dispersal of Debbie's clothes, and so much other stuff that had me buried, trapped me, caused me to be unable to breathe. Stuff reeking of too many wonderful and painful memories. Stuff that keeps me from letting her go—prevents me from being okay. I must disconnect, let her go, release my grip on the precious pain I horde, and cling to, like Gollum, the *one ring*. I must stop holding my breath, waiting for Debbie to take another gulp of air. I must diverge. I must choose life, and joy, and love. I promised.

"You're drinking too much," I hear Debbie say.

I know.

"Just don't forget me."

Like that's even possible, babe.

# GREAT BANQUET TALK 2008

### By Debbie Wilson

"My name is Debbie Wilson, and I want to talk to you about a life of Christian action.

"I can guess what you might be thinking right now. A life of Christian action means I must *do* something. People are going to expect me to participate in 'church stuff.' I'm so busy; how can I possibly fit one more thing into my schedule?

"A life of Christian action is much more than just going through the motions. Motion is *talking* about changing reality. Action is *doing* what it takes to change reality.

"I was twenty-one years old when I married my husband, Chuck; young by today's standards. I had been raised in the church, had a church wedding, but had mixed feelings about God. I believed in a God, but he cramped my style. I didn't think God and 'fun' were synonymous. So, I wasn't too bothered by the fact that my husband, Chuck, had no interest in organized religion.

"It wasn't until we had children that I began to reassess my perception. I wanted my children to have what I had as a child—the weekly ritual of Sunday school, followed by meals at my grandmother's where my cousins and I ran wild, our parents gathered around the table to sip coffee. Chuck didn't buy into my Norman Rockwell ideal, but I talked him into attending a small country church not far from where we lived.

"Our lives were busy. Church became a casualty of our hectic lifestyle. The hit-and-miss approach to worship became a source of tension, and I complained to a Christian neighbor about Chuck's indifference. She told me the story of how she prayed for her alcoholic husband, and how it changed their lives. She claimed he was 'born again.'

"When I snidely remarked that Chuck would never pray with me the way her husband prayed with her, she replied, 'God can do anything; you must have faith, know that God is listening, and wait patiently for his answer.' She emphatically urged me to pray for him.

"I decided to give it a shot. I went home, got on my knees, and prayed to God to transform our lives. I wanted our home to be Christ-centered. I got up from my prayer, and waited for the miracle.

"But nothing happened. Chuck remained the same, I didn't change, and we continued as before. After a few weeks, that prayer was a distant memory.

"Months passed. At the end of 1987, my husband had a brand-new MBA, was job hunting, and we had just put our house on the market. Black Monday hit, and overnight, businesses were in a hiring freeze. Then, just weeks later, I discovered a lump in my breast. That lump was breast cancer.

"Did I turn to God for strength and comfort? No. I was angry. I blamed God. I was convinced he was punishing us because we hadn't been to church in months.

"We put our possessions in storage, and accepted an offer from a friend to stay with her. It was in this setting that I discovered God's unconditional love for me.

"That same friend asked my local minister to speak with me and—even though it was against my wishes—he chose *action*. He came to visit me, and listened attentively as I opened a floodgate of emotions. Through my tears, I told him I didn't deserve God's love. The pastor took my hands, looked in my eyes, and assured me God would give me strength to get through the following days and months.

"Two years after that, I found myself back in the same hospital, experiencing the same feelings of helplessness, fear, and uncertainty. I don't remember the name of the young lady who shared my hospital room during that time, but I do remember what she did for me: she prayed.

She identified a need, and went into *action*. She overlooked her own pain in order to help me through mine.

"This new cancer was rare—only two in a million per year in the U.S. are diagnosed with it. It marked the beginning of a very long journey. To share all my subsequent cancer encounters would take more time than we have. Let's just say that after the adrenal cancer there were lung and liver metastases; the removal of ninety percent of my liver; two more breast cancers; a chest wall sarcoma; several lung surgeries, and lymphoma. Recent genetic tests have confirmed I carry a mutated gene that predisposes me to cancer.

"I've also undergone grueling clinical trials that required almost one hundred hours of chemotherapy infusion. I lost all my hair, had sores in my mouth, my bones ached, and the skin peeled off the bottom of my feet. There were times I didn't think I could endure any more, but the *actions* of kindness and prayer from family, friends, and strangers saw me through.

"I share this with you because I want you to understand that the 'life of Christian action' is how God's grace comes *alive* for people—and you don't have to drop everything and become a missionary in a remote area of the world for that to happen.

"During one of those trials, Christmas was approaching and I had neither the desire nor energy to put up a tree. I boarded the plane to go home feeling sad and very alone. As my husband and I pulled into our driveway, he jumped out and shouted, 'Wait a minute, I'll be right back.' He ran into the garage. Suddenly, the house was ablaze with Christmas lights.

"I was bowled over. He led me into the house where I was in for an even *bigger* surprise: the entire house was decorated, right down to mistletoe in the doorway. Chuck told me that friends from our Tennessee church had arrived at our house on a mission: they were going to decorate our home for Christmas, and boy, they did—big time. They chose action.

"These same friends regularly brought meals when I was too sick to get out of bed. One of them drove to the house twice a week to draw blood for tests, so that I wouldn't have to take trips to the local hospital. Can you see how these actions helped us see God more clearly?

"As odd as it sounds, cancer was one of our greatest blessings. It brought us both to Christ. Yes, even Chuck realized who ultimately is in control. What a privilege it is for us to now give to others what God has given us.

"Difficulties are bound to arise, but never forget that God is at work—even in our failures, and even in our trials. Romans 8:28 says: 'We know that in all things God works for the good of those who love him, who have been called according to his purpose' (NIV).

"You may wonder how I personally live a life of Christian action. I endeavor to do that which I laid out for you in my talk. I pray. I knit prayer shawls for those in need of comfort. I accepted an invitation to become a deacon in my church.

"I also try, whenever possible, to share my story with others, hoping that they will see my faith journey, and want to begin one of their own.

"St. Francis of Assisi said, 'Preach Christ at all times; if necessary, use words.' Today I used many words, and I pray that those words will encourage you to consider living a grace-based life.

"Choose action. Choose Christ's love. Choose to pray for those around you, and to accept the prayer and help of others. Choose faith, to believe God's promises to you, even when they seem impossible. Choose to actively pass that legacy on to your children and your children's children. If you have undergone great trials, as I have, choose to share your story. If it were not for the choices and actions of others, I would not be at this podium tonight. There will undoubtedly be others who will one day say the same things of you—if you choose action. "

# BRIEF MEDICAL HISTORY

- **11/87** - (L) breast carcinoma (intraductal): left breast segmentectomy & left axillary node dissection followed by radiation, and adjuvant (CMF) chemotherapy
  - Dr. Thomas E. Penn, Genesee Hospital, Rochester NY
- **9/89** - (L) adrenal cortical carcinoma (ACC)(non-functioning); (L) adrenalectomy, (L) nephrectomy, splenectomy.
  - **Told to get my affairs in order (1ˢᵗ time).**
  - Dr. Thomas E. Penn, Genesee Hospital, Rochester, NY
- **5/90** - (R) lung metastasis; thoracotomy to remove "coin lesion" (diagnosed as adrenal metastatic lesion)
  - Dr. Robert Leyse, Long Beach Naval Hospital, Long Beach, CA
- **5/91** - Intraductal breast carcinoma, (R) breast: multifocal intraductal carcinoma with multiple foci of micro-invasive ductal carcinoma: lumpectomy, external radiation therapy, followed by interstitial iridium implant
  - Dr. Anthony Ciarolla, MD, Long Beach, CA
  - Dr. Ajmel A. Puthawala, California Radiation Oncology Medical Group, Inc., Long Beach, CA
- **9/92** - Bilateral mastectomy followed by breast reconstruction
  - Dr. Davis Bronson, Grossmont Hospital, La Mesa, CA
- **8/93** – Scans indicate over a dozen tumors throughout my liver.
  - **Told to get my affairs in order (2ⁿᵈ time)**

- **10/93** - Left thoracotomy for suspicious lesions – benign
- **8/94** - Exploratory laparotomy – small nodule removed from liver – metastatic adrenal carcinoma
  - Dr. Maureen Martin, University of Iowa Medical Center, Iowa City, IA
- **3/95** - Right chest wall tumor excision – malignant fibrous histiocytoma (MFH)
  - Dr. Peter Jochimsem, University of Iowa Medical Center, Iowa City, IA
- **4/95** - Wide local excision of scar from 3/95 surgery. No evidence of cancer
- **3/97** - Widespread metastatic adrenal cortical carcinoma to the liver: Right trisegmentectomy with tube thoracotomy, 90% of liver removed (seven of eight lobes). Survival deemed very unlikely. Family called in.
  - **I count this as the <u>third time</u> I needed to get my affairs in order.**
  - Dr. Maureen Martin, University of Iowa Medical Center, Iowa City, IA
- **1/99** - Fluid around left lung drained twice. Adrenal cancer cells detected in fluid – pleurodesis performed.
  - Dr. E. B. Golden, Jr., Memphis Lung Physicians, Memphis, TN
- **6/00** - Metastatic liver lesion (adrenal); radio-frequency ablation
  - Dr. Maureen Martin, Beth Israel Deaconess Hospital, Boston, MA
  - Dr. Nahem Goldberg, Beth Israel Deaconess Hospital, Boston, MA
- **8/00** - Unsuccessful parathyroid surgery: pathology determines tissue removed by surgeon to be "brown fat" misidentified during procedure as parathyroid tissue. Procedure must be redone at some future time
  - Dr. Stanley L. Smith, Baptist Hospital East, Memphis, TN
- **10/00** - Large tumor near left breast implant; resection (benign)

-Dr. George L. Burruss, Plastic Surgery Group, Memphis, TN

- **9/01** - Metastatic Liver tumor (adrenal); radio-frequency (RF) (open) ablation

-Dr. Ravi Chari, Vanderbilt Medical Center, Nashville, TN

(Near fatal episode due to abscess from RF ablation to liver results in hospital admission for antibiotic therapy, drainage tube

-Baptist East Hospital, Memphis, TN)

- **6/02** - Positive pap test – cryo-treatment
  - Dr. Lawrence Johnson, Memphis, TN

- **10/03** – Scans reveal that tumors have returned to my liver. This time they are located too close to only remaining blood supply for either RF ablation or surgery to be an option.
  - With no proven chemotherapy for adrenal cortical carcinoma, Dr. Weir, my oncologist, **advises me to get my affairs in order (4<u>th</u> time)**.
  - With Dr. Weir's help, I begin searching for medical trials that might offer hope and am soon accepted into a study at the National Institutes of Health in Bethesda, MD.
  - Dr. Al B. Weir, Memphis, TN

- **11/03** - Began experimental chemotherapy – anti-angiogenesis inhibitor at National Institutes of Health (NIH), Bethesda, MD. Participated until 3/04 – treatment determined to be ineffective. However, a Medical trial specifically focused on adrenal cancer has begun. I must wait for the chemicals from the first trial to clear out of my system and have other medical tests performed to ensure I am a candidate for the study.

- **4/04** - April – Began experimental study targeting adrenal cortical carcinoma with MAVE (mitotane, adriamycin, vincrinstine, etoposide) + tariquidor
  - Dr. Tito Fojo, National Institutes of Health, Bethesda, MD.

- **4/04** – Insertion of port-a-catheter – NIH

- **11/04** – Fell and fractured left fibula

- **3/05** – Chemotherapy ends. Positive results – shrinkage of tumors. Dr. Fojo states that while there was significant shrinkage of the tumors, cancer will return and there will be nothing further that can be done. He recommends moving near family for help "at the end."
  - **Fifth time I am told to get my affairs in order.**
  - Decision made to move to Florida to be near my sister, Nancy Keefer for support.
- **5/05** – Benign skin lesion removed from back (right flank)
- **8/05** – Bilateral breast explantation/implantation (due to ruptured saline implant)
  - Dr. Larry Lichstein, Cleveland Clinic, Naples, FL
- **10/05** – Renal stone (R kidney) lithotripsy
  - Dr. Scappa
- **1/06** - Removal of port-a-catheter (NIH Bethesda, MD)
- **3/06** – Basal cell carcinoma (right side temporal scalp), compound nevus with mild architectural atypia, excised (left lateral upper back), basal cell carcinoma (left costal margin) ...
  - Javier Lugo, MD, Naples, FL
- **5/07** – Basal cell on scalp...removed (scraped, and cauterized)
  - Dr. Gregory M. Houck, Estero Dermatology, Estero, FL
- **9/07** – Third breast cancer occurs in remaining microscopic breast tissue cells under right arm...tumor surgically removed at NIH. ER/PR Positive... Tamoxifen regimen begun: 20mg per day.
- **11/07** – Mole removed from left side... "atypical" ...further surgery removed margins...okay
- **12/07** – Two moles removed from left abdomen... "atypical" ... will follow up with more surgery to check margins.
- **1/2/08** – Mole removed from right side (towards back), "atypical" ...further surgery removed margins...okay
- **2/5/08** – Parathyroid surgery, NIH, one parathyroid gland removed – success!

- Dr. Mary Beth Hughes.
- **6/20/08** – Needle aspiration of seroma surrounding right breast implant. Malignant cells found. Pathology sent to NIH for further analysis.
  - Dr. Wm. Kokal, Fort Myers, FL.
- **7/08/08** – surgical removal of right breast implant.

### ***Genetic test results received from NIH: Li-Fraumeni Syndrome***

**Li-Fraumeni Syndrome is extremely rare and predisposes those with it to developing cancer. It is great to finally have an explanation for my continuous onslaught of various malignancies, but each of my sons has a 50% probability of inheriting this genetic defect. Brian tests negative. Greg has yet to be tested.**

- **8/08** – Staph infection to site of 7/08/08 surgery.... cleaned, and closed.
  - Dr. Justin Warner, Naples, FL.
- **9/08** – Needle aspiration of fluid around left lung...NIH (no cancer cells)
- **10/08** – Hysterectomy
  - Dr. Edward Grendys, Lee Memorial Hospital, Fort Myers, FL.
- **5/09** – DIEP Flap reconstruction (healing issues with abdominal scar – wound vacuum used from 5/09-9/09)
  - Dr. Minas Chrysopoulo, Methodist Hospital, San Antonio, TX
- **10/09** – Scar revision, nipple construction.
- **1/10** – Nipple tattooing
- **12/10** – Whipple procedure, and liver resection (ampullary carcinoma; adrenal tumor in liver). I become the twenty-seventh person in U.S. history to have had these two major medical procedures combined during a single surgery. Every doctor

involved during the fourteen-hour surgery says it was the most difficult surgery of their career.

- Dr. Itzhak Avital, National Institutes of Health, Bethesda, MD.

- **7/11** – Liver ablation.

  - Dr. Nadine Abi-Jaoudeh, NIH, Bethesda, MD

- **2/12-6/12** – Chemotherapy for liver tumor: cisplatin, 73 mm (14 infusions).

  - Dr. Valiant D. Tan, Virginia Oncology, Chesapeake, VA.

- **11/12** – Heart ablation

  - Dr. Woollett: Sentara Heart Hospital, Norfolk, VA.

- **07/13** – MOHS surgery on nose and head

  - Dr. Lawrence K. Chang.

  Closure of head incision and skin graft to nose

  - Dr. Richard S. Rosenblum.

- **9/13** – Biopsies of chest wall lesions and multiple retroperitoneal nodes. Chest wall lesions positive for adrenal metastases. Nodes inconclusive. Dr. Fojo suspects lymphoma.

- **1/14** – Blood tests (1/10/13) indicate abnormal WBC. Extra tests performed. Diagnosis: chronic lymphocytic leukemia (CLL).

- **1/10** - CT scan shows five lesions on chest wall; four are the same or slightly larger than previous scan and one is two times larger. Tumors assumed to be adrenal cancer. Lymph nodes in retroperitoneum are enlarged. Blood drawn to look at CD 20 receptor to determine if Retuximab treatment appropriate.

- **1/14** – Things are more "complicated" than originally thought. I am referred to Lymphoid Malignancies Section Hematology Branch, NIH (Dr. Adrian Wiestner).

- **3/14** – Begin last-ditch chemotherapy: Doxil.

- **5/7/14** – 911 called due to hyperventilating, high fever, uncontrollable shaking. Determined to be septic. Admitted to hospital. E-Coli infection.
  - Chesapeake General Hospital
- **7/8/14** – Chemo determined to be ineffective. Decision made to stop all treatments.
  - **Advised by NIH medical team to begin relationship with hospice and get my affairs in order (6ᵗʰ and final time).**
- **7/25/14** – Right lung collapses due to tumor activity blocking airway while in New York for fortieth high school class reunion. Debbie unwilling to go to local ER. Travel five hours to NIH where she is admitted in very frail condition. Possibility of installing stent to reopen airway considered but determined to not be worthwhile. Return home after week in hospital with intention to soon begin relationship with hospice.
- **8/5/14** – 911 called due to explosive and massive release of blood and material from blocked lung. Released a day later as there is nothing to be done but begin hospice care.
- **8/9/14** – Begin relationship with hospice organization recommended by Dr. Rosemary Balderston, Family Medicine Physician, Chesapeake, VA. Superb care received from her nurses, Monica Burns, RN and Barbara Ramirez, LPN.
  - Medi Home Health & Hospice, Chesapeake, VA
- **12/11/14** – Having survived longer with adrenal cortical carcinoma than anyone in known history and experiencing ten primary cancers, possibly another record, Debbie passes away at home with family at her side.